¡Viva el Español!

Ava Belisle-Chatterjee
Linda West Tibensky
Abraham Martínez-Cruz

National Textbook Company

a division of NTC/CONTEMPORARY PUBLISHING GROUP
Lincolnwood, Illinois USA

Project Director: *Keith Fry*
Project Managers: *William Hrabrick, Frank Crane*
                            Publishing Services International, Inc.
Contributing Writer: *Judy Veramendi*
Design Concept: *Rosa + Wesley Design Associates*
Cover Design: *Rosa + Wesley Design Associates*
Page Design: *Fulcrum Creative*
Art & Production Coordinator: *Nancy Ellis*
Cover Photographer: *Robert Keeling*
Cover Illustrator: *Terri Starrett*
Illustrators: *Tim Basaldua, James Buckley, Mickey Gill,*
Carolyn Gruber, Nancy Panacionne, Leanne Thomas,
Don Wilson, Fred Womack

Acknowledgments appear on page 247, which is to be considered
an extension of this copyright page.

ISBN: 0-8442-0943-0

Published by National Textbook Company,
a division of NTC/Contemporary Publishing Group, Inc.,
4255 West Touhy Avenue,
Lincolnwood (Chicago), Illinois 60712-1975 U.S.A.

99 00 01 02 03 04 05 06 07 08 09   QB   0 9 8 7 6 5

CONTENTS

Unidad 3

Unidad 4

Appendix

¡Viva el Español!

¡BIENVENIDOS!

That means "welcome"! This year you're going to have some new and exciting experiences as you explore the world of Spanish!

From the beginning, you'll be learning to say things the way people say them in countries like Argentina, Spain, and Mexico…and you'll be able to use your Spanish to talk to people in your own city or town, or even in your own school!

So, welcome to school, and join with your classmates in saying **¡Viva el español!**

In these first lessons, you'll:

- Learn how to say hello and good-bye
- Talk about how you feel
- Name different objects in your classroom
- Use numbers to do everyday things

Estas niñas son amigas.

¡Hola, Luis!

En un parque de
San Sebastián, España

¡HABLEMOS!

What's your name?

¿Cómo te llamas?

Me llamo Teresa.

¿Cómo se llama el muchacho?

Se llama Ernesto.

¿Cómo se llama la muchacha?

Se llama Rosa.

Clase, me llamo señorita Rivera.

Why not choose a Spanish name for yourself? It can be the Spanish version of your name, if there is one, or a brand new name that you like. You can use it during Spanish class—and afterward. There is a list of names on pages 228-229 of this book. Your teacher may have some suggestions, also.

PRACTIQUEMOS

Six boys and girls are waiting to meet with you after school. Look at their names and faces. Then answer the questions.

—¿Cómo se llama el muchacho?

—Se llama Ernesto.

1.  ¿Cómo se llama la muchacha?

Se llama ~~Ana~~ Rosa

2. ¿Cómo se llama el muchacho?

Se llama Ernesto

3.  ¿Cómo se llama la muchacha?

Se llama Isabel

4. ¿Cómo se llama la muchacha?

se llama Rosa

5.  ¿Cómo se llama el muchacho?

se llama Carlos

6. ¿Cómo te llamas tú?

Brianna

¡HABLEMOS!

Hello and good-bye

PRACTIQUEMOS

A. Choose a partner. Practice greeting each other, and then saying good-bye. (Be careful—more than one answer may be correct.)

PARTNER A: Say what is in the picture.
PARTNER B: Answer with an appropriate response.

—¡Buenas noches!
—**¡Buenas noches!** OR **¡Hasta mañana!** OR **¡Adiós!**

1.
   Buenas tardes.

2.
   ¿Cómo estás?

3.
   ¡Adiós!

4.
   Buenos días.

5.
   ¿Cómo estás?

6.
   ¡Hasta luego!

B. How do your friends feel? Look at the picture on the top of page 5 to see. Take the part of each friend as you answer the questions.

—¿Cómo estás, Ernesto?

—**Estoy muy mal.** OR **Muy mal.**

1. ¿Cómo estás, Rosa? **4.** ¿Cómo estás, Isabel?

2. ¿Cómo estás, José? **5.** ¿Cómo estás, Carlos?

3. ¿Cómo estás, Ana?

Now ask some of your own classmates: **¿Cómo estás tú?**

Brianna

¿Cómo estás, amigo?

ENTRE AMIGOS

Entre amigos means "among friends." Whenever you see an **Entre amigos** activity, you know you're going to have fun. These activities let you use Spanish to talk with your classmates in pairs and larger groups. Here's a good example:

Play a game with your class. Write your name on five index cards. Put the cards in a box with your classmates' cards. Mix them up, then draw five cards. (If you draw a card with your own name, put it back and take a new card.)

Walk around the classroom asking **¿Cómo te llamas?** When you find the owner of the name on one of your cards, give it back. The first person to return all the cards wins.

¿Cómo te llamas?

¡HABLEMOS!

What's this?

—¿Qué es esto? ¿Es una pizarra?

—No. Es una puerta.

un escritorio

una pizarra

un pupitre

una silla

una puerta

una luz

una computadora

PRACTIQUEMOS

Work with a partner. Ask and answer questions about things in the classroom.

PARTNER A: Ask what the item in the picture is.
PARTNER B: Say what the item is.

—¿Qué es esto?

—Es una silla.

 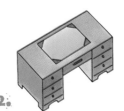 

1.   2.   3.

4.   5.   6.

ENTRE AMIGOS

Get together in a group of three or four classmates and ask each other questions about things in your own classroom. One person points to something and asks what it is. The other person answers.

¡HABLEMOS!

Who is that?

¿Quién es?

Es el profesor.

El profesor es un hombre.

el profesor

La profesora es una mujer.

la profesora

Un alumno es un muchacho.

un alumno

Una alumna es una muchacha.

una alumna

¿Es un alumno?

PRACTIQUEMOS

 **A.** Get together with a partner. Ask and answer each other's questions about different people.

PARTNER A: Ask the question.
PARTNER B: Look at the picture and answer.

—¿Quién es?

—Es un alumno.

 1.

 2.

 3.

Now ask each other the same question about different people in your classroom!

B. You want a tutor to help you learn the new words. Work with a partner, who will play the tutor. Your tutor asks the question and you respond with the correct answer.

—¿Es un pupitre?

—No. Es una puerta.

1.

¿Es una computadora?

2.

¿Es una pizarra?

3.

¿Es una profesora?

4.

¿Es un profesor?

C. Work with a partner. Ask and answer each other's questions about the picture using **¿Qué es esto?** or **¿Quién es?** Together, make a list of the people and things you see.

ENTRE AMIGOS

Get together with a partner. Make four cards with the question **¿Quién es?** and four cards with the question **¿Qué es esto?** Mix them up, then spread them out face down on your desk.

Now make cards with pictures of the items and people in this lesson. Mix them up, then spread them out face down on your partner's desk.

Pick a question card and ask the question; then pick a picture card and respond. If the question matches the answer, keep the pair. If not, return both cards to their original positions.

Take turns. Play until there are no more question cards on the desk. The player with the most pairs wins.

¿Cuáles son los números?

¡HABLEMOS!

Numbers from 1 to 10

—¿Cuál es el número?

—Es el siete.

0	cero	6	seis
1	uno	7	siete
2	dos	8	ocho
3	tres	9	nueve
4	cuatro	10	diez
5	cinco		

Numbers from 11 to 20

— ¿Es el doce?

— No. Es el diecinueve.

11	once	16	dieciséis
12	doce	17	diecisiete
13	trece	18	dieciocho
14	catorce	19	diecinueve
15	quince	20	veinte

Numbers from 21 to 29

— ¿Qué número es?

— Es el veinticuatro.

21	veintiuno	26	veintiséis
22	veintidós	27	veintisiete
23	veintitrés	28	veintiocho
24	veinticuatro	29	veintinueve
25	veinticinco		

PRACTIQUEMOS

Imagine that you are a judge at a bicycle race. As the contestants pass by, you must say who has what number.

Look at each picture. Say what number the person is.

José
12
José: doce

Anita
25
1.

Emilio
5
2.

Pepe
11
3.

Julio
14
4.

Luis
15
5.

Olivia
10
6.

María
18
7.

Adela
22
8.

Clara
13
9.

Lupe
20
10.

Gloria
3
11.

Daniel
29
12.

¡HABLEMOS!

All kinds of numbers

A. Work with a partner. Take turns asking each other questions about different friends' phone numbers.

PARTNER A: Ask for the phone number of the people listed.

PARTNER B: Say the phone number.

—¿Cuál es el número de teléfono de Ana Méndez?

—Es el ocho, dos, cuatro, siete, cuatro, tres, dos.

Nombre	Número
Arturo Castillo	332-5681
Beto Chávez	482-7805
Elena Gómez	264-1539
Margarita Luna	995-6217
Ana Méndez	824-7432
Tomás Pérez	553-4760
Victoria Silva	761-8849

Un teléfono público

B. You and a friend are working on some math problems in Spanish.

> **PARTNER A:** Look at the problem and ask what the answer is.
>
> **PARTNER B:** Say the problem and the answer.

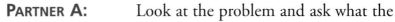

4 + 6 =   —¿Cuántos son cuatro más seis?

—Cuatro más seis son diez.

1. 6 + 8 =
2. 5 + 5 =
3. 20 + 8 =
4. 7 + 9 =
5. 13 + 4 =

6. 19 + 1 =
7. 23 + 4 =
8. 11 + 4 =
9. 6 + 6 =
10. 17 + 5 =

ENTRE AMIGOS

 Look up the phone number of an important or interesting place in your community and bring the number to school. (It could be the number of the fire department, for example, or the number of your favorite department store.)

Get together with four or five classmates, tell the name of the place you choose, and give the phone number—in Spanish, of course!

Put your group's list on the classroom wall. The other groups in your class will do the same. That way, you can copy down any number you want and keep it in your own directory.

El salón de clase

Can you close your eyes and name all the things in your classroom? How long would it take you?

It's easy to remember names of things we use every day. And remembering their names in Spanish is just as easy. In this unit, you'll:

- Name classroom objects and school supplies
- Talk about one person or thing, or several
- Talk about friends
- Learn about classrooms in Spanish-speaking countries

Alumnas en Guatemala

Alumnos en Chile

Una alumna cubana en Miami

¿Sabes que...?

- In many schools in Spain and Latin America, students wear uniforms.

- In many Spanish-speaking countries, classrooms have 40 to 50 students.

- In most schools in Spanish-speaking countries, students buy their own books—even in public schools.

- Some schools in Spain and Latin America are very old. El Colegio Mayor de Nuestra Señora del Rosario in Bogotá, Colombia, is over 250 years old.

¡HABLEMOS!

What is it?

—¿Qué es esto?

—Es el salón de clase.

el salón de clase

el reloj

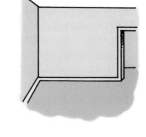

la pared

la bandera

el globo

la ventana

el borrador

la mesa

el mapa

la cesta

la tiza

Así es... Did you know that the Spanish word *mesa* is also an English word? In English, a mesa is a high, rocky hill with a flat top. There are lots of them in the southwestern United States—in places like Mesa, Arizona, or Mesa Verde National Park in Colorado.

Practiquemos

 You're helping a new student in class to name different classroom objects in Spanish.

PARTNER A: Ask what each object is.
PARTNER B: Name the object.

—¿Qué es esto?

—Es el mapa.

1.

2.

3.

4.

5.

6.

7.

8.

9.

ENTRE AMIGOS

Are you a good guesser? Here's a chance to find out. Take a piece of paper. Fold it in half, then in half again. Open the paper; then cut or tear it along the folds to make four smaller pieces. On each piece, write the name of a different classroom object in Spanish.

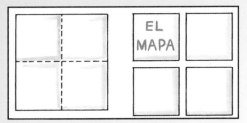

Now get together with a partner, who also has four pieces of paper. Put one piece of paper face down in front of your partner. Say:

¿Qué es esto?

Without turning the paper over, your partner has to guess what is written on it:

Es (el mapa).

If **el mapa** is the word on your paper, your partner gets one point. But if it isn't, you say something like:

No. Es (la ventana).

Then *you* get one point. The person with the most points after two minutes is the winner. Change partners for another game.

¡HABLEMOS!

What's on the desk?

—¿Qué hay en el pupitre?
—Hay un cuaderno.

un cuaderno

un lápiz   **una hoja de papel**

Una clase en Colombia.

—¿Tienes un libro?
—Sí, claro.

un libro

una regla

un bolígrafo

Así es... In Latin America, many schools are actually two schools in one! One group of students comes in the morning. The other group comes in the afternoon, uses the same classrooms, and works until evening. Even the teachers are different!

PRACTIQUEMOS

 You need to borrow some things for a school project, so you call a friend.

PARTNER A: Ask a question based on the picture.
PARTNER B: Answer the question.

—**¿Tienes una regla?**

—**Sí.** OR **Sí, claro.**

1.

2.

3.

4.

ENTRE AMIGOS

 What school supplies do you have in or on your desk?
How about your classmates?

Work with a partner. Ask your partner the following questions:

¿Tienes un lápiz en el pupitre?
¿Tienes un cuaderno en el pupitre?
¿Tienes una regla en el pupitre?
¿Tienes un bolígrafo en el pupitre?
¿Tienes un libro en el pupitre?
¿Tienes una hoja de papel en el pupitre?

Your partner responds based on what he or she has:

¡Sí, claro! OR **No.**

Then your partner asks you the same questions.

¿CÓMO LO DICES?

Talking about more than one

Look at these words. How do they change when there is more than one?

un globo

dos globos

una mesa

dos mesas

In Spanish, words that end in the letters **a, e, i, o,** or **u** add the letter **-s** when we talk about more than one.

Now look at these words. How do they change when there is more than one?

un
profesor

dos
profesores

un reloj

dos relojes

In Spanish, words that *don't* end in **a, e, i, o,** or **u** add the letters **-es** when we talk about more than one.

If you want to ask how many there are of something, you say **¿Cuántos hay?** or **¿Cuántas hay?**

—¿Cuántos bolígrafos hay?   —¿Cuántas sillas hay?
—Hay dos.   —Hay veinticuatro.

You use **cuántos** with words that use **el,** and **cuántas** with words that use **la.**

¿Cuántas alumnas hay?

¡Úsalo!

A. Look at each picture. When your partner asks, how quickly can you answer?

PARTNER A: Ask about the amount that is there.
PARTNER B: Answer "yes" or "no" based on the picture.

—¿Hay tres cuadernos?

—**No.**

1.  ¿Hay tres globos?

2.  ¿Hay dos profesores?

3.  ¿Hay cuatro borradores?

4.  ¿Hay dos pupitres?

¿Hay una profesora en el salón de clase?

B. Imagine that you have to count everything in the classroom, including the people! Follow the example.

el borrador – 12
Hay doce borradores.

1. la pared – 4

2. el alumno – 18

3. el profesor – 1

4. la silla – 28

5. la regla – 22

6. el pupitre – 19

7. la puerta – 1

8. la alumna – 14

9. el globo – 3

C. For each item, tell how many there are.

Hay tres relojes.

1.

2.

3.

4.

5.

6.

ENTRE AMIGOS

Write the answers to these questions about your classroom. Questions 5 and 6 have blanks so that you can put in names of things you are curious about—for example: **globos, reglas, borradores, tizas.** Don't look around or try to count—just give your best guess.

1. ¿Cuántos alumnos hay?

2. ¿Cuántas alumnas hay?

3. ¿Cuántos profesores hay?

4. ¿Cuántos relojes hay?

5. ¿Cuántos _____ hay?

6. ¿Cuántas _____ hay?

Get in a group of three classmates. Ask one another the questions. Are your answers the same or different? If they are different, is it by a lot or a little?

¿Cómo lo dices?

Talking about people and things

Look at the examples. Notice how the words **el** and **la** change when you talk about more than one person.

el alumno

los alumnos

la alumna

las alumnas

Notice how **el** and **la** change when you talk about more than one thing:

el cuaderno

los cuadernos

la bandera

las banderas

Did you notice that **el** changes to **los** and **la** changes to **las** when you talk about more than one person or thing?

When you want to know what something is, you ask **¿Qué es esto?** To ask about more than one thing, use the question **¿Qué son estos?** When you want to know who someone is, you ask **¿Quién es?** and when you want to know who several or many people are, you ask **¿Quiénes son?**

¡ÚSALO!

A. You're helping to put supplies and furniture in your classroom.

PARTNER A: Ask what your partner has.
PARTNER B: Answer according to the picture.

—¿Qué tienes?

—Los cuadernos.

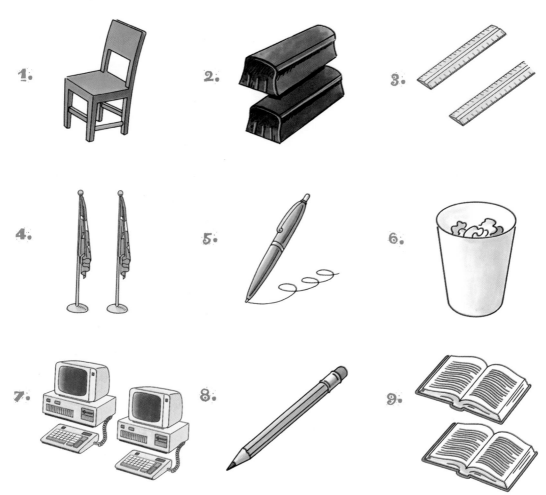

1.

2.

3.

4.

5.

6.

7.

8.

9.

Una lección en clase

B. A visiting student from Madrid is showing you pictures of typical Spanish classrooms, and you have some questions.

PARTNER A: Ask what the item or person is.
PARTNER B: Answer according to the picture.

—¿Qué es esto?
—**Es el cuaderno.**

1. ¿Qué son estos?   2. ¿Quién es?   3. ¿Qué es esto?

4. ¿Qué son estos?   5. ¿Qué es esto?   6. ¿Quiénes son?

Los alumnos escriben en los cuadernos.

ENTRE AMIGOS

Play a guessing game with a partner. Tell your partner to close his or her eyes. Then get an object (or objects) from your desk or from some other place in the room, and have your partner touch it (or touch them). As your partner is touching the item(s), you ask:

¿Qué es esto? OR **¿Qué son estos?**

Your partner has to say the right answer:

Es (un lápiz). OR **Son (las tizas).**

Do this five times, then change roles with your partner.

¡A divertirnos!

Now play a game with the names of all the classroom objects and school supplies you know.

You and each of your classmates will take one index card and write on it the name of an object—or objects—in the class. For example, you can write **un bolígrafo** or something longer like **cuatro borradores.**

Ask your teacher to collect all the cards, shuffle them and put them face down on a table or desk.

Now make two teams of all your classmates. To play, members of each team take turns picking a card, reading it aloud, and then pointing to the object(s) it describes. If a team member is correct, his or her team gets a point. If the team member is not correct, the other team gets a point.

The first team to get 20 points is the winner. **¡Buena suerte**!—good luck!

Ánimales de varios colores

Do you have any pets? Do your classmates have pets?

If you and your classmates were to put on an animal show, your pets would probably be all different sizes, shapes, and colors. There are even more sizes, shapes, and colors in the world of wild animals.

In this unit, you're going to:

- Learn the names of colors and shapes
- Identify different animals
- Describe your pets and other favorite animals
- Find out about some South American animals

Éste es el pájaro bobo de patas azules. Es de las Islas Galápagos, Ecuador.

¿Cómo son los flamencos?

¿Sabes que...?

- The largest snake in the world is the South American anaconda. It can grow to 30 feet.

- The Galápagos Islands off the coast of Ecuador are home to some of the most unusual animals in the world.

- The black panther of the Central American jungle is really a jaguar whose spots you can't see.

Unas llamas en los Andes

¡HABLEMOS!

What color is it?

—¿De qué color es?
—Es rojo.

rojo

verde

amarillo

anaranjado

rosado

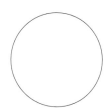

blanco

azul

morado

negro

gris

marrón

—¿Qué es esto?
—Es un triángulo. Es azul.

el triángulo

el rectángulo

el cuadrado

el círculo

Así es...

As you travel from country to country in the Spanish-speaking world, you will hear many different words for the color "brown": *castaño, café, marrón,* and *pardo* are just a few. You don't have to learn all of these now, but be aware that some words are different in different countries.

PRACTIQUEMOS

A. A friend's little brother is having trouble remembering the colors. Look at each picture and tell him what color the item is.

Es anaranjado.

1.
2.
3.
4.

5.
6.
7.
8.

¿De qué color es la tortuga?

B. Practice talking about shapes and colors with a partner.

PARTNER A: Look at the shape and ask its color.
PARTNER B: Say what color the shape is.

 —¿De qué color es el triángulo?
—Es verde.

 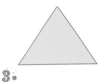

1.   2.   3.   4.

5.   6.   7.   8.

ENTRE AMIGOS

On a piece of paper make four columns, each headed by one of these color words: **verde, marrón, azul, gris.** Now look around your classroom for objects that are these colors. Write the Spanish word for each item in the correct column.

Then with a partner take turns pointing to one of the objects that is on your list and asking what color it is.

—¿De qué color es la pizarra?
—Es verde.
—¿De qué color es el lápiz?
—Es marrón.

¡HABLEMOS!

What's your favorite animal?

—¿Qué animal es?
—Es un gato.
—¿De qué color es?
—Es marrón.

el gato

el pájaro

el canario

el loro

el tigre

el ratón

la mariposa

el flamenco

el conejo

—¿¿Cuál es tu animal favorito?
—El perro.

el perro

el pez

Este coquí es puertorriqueño.

el oso

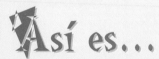 **Así es...**

The *coquí*, a small tree frog, lives in Puerto Rico. The *coquí* gets its name from the distinctive sound it makes as it calls to other frogs: *coquí, coquí, coquí.* You wouldn't believe such a small animal could make so much noise!

PRACTIQUEMOS

A. Your class is taking a trip to the zoo. You and a friend are walking around talking about the animals—in Spanish.

PARTNER A: Ask what animal it is.
PARTNER B: Look at the picture and answer.

—¿Qué animal es?
—Es un loro.

1.
2.
3.
4.

5.
6.
7.
8.

Estos animales son iguanas.

B. You and your friend are in a pet shop. Ask your friend what color the different animals are.

—¿De qué color es?
—Es gris.

1.

2.

3.

4.

5.

6.

7.

8.

ENTRE AMIGOS

 Play a game with a partner. Write down the Spanish name of an animal, but don't show it to your partner. Then ask your partner: **¿Qué animal es?**

Your partner has to guess the animal **(Es un _____)**. Your partner has two chances to guess the animal, and receives a point for a correct answer.

Then your partner takes a turn writing the name of an animal and asking the question. Keep playing until one of you reaches five points. That person is the winner.

¿Cómo lo dices?

Describing things

Colors are one way to describe things. Look at these sentences to see how to say that different things are yellow.

El canario es amarill**o**.

La luz es amarill**a**.

La mariposa es amarill**a**.

Did you notice that sometimes the word is **amarill*o*** and sometimes it's **amarill*a*?** Many descriptive words end in **-o** or **-a** (like **amarillo** and **amarilla**). These descriptive words end in **-o** with words that use **el.** They end in **-a** with words that use **la.**

A lot of descriptive words don't end in **-o** or **-a.** Look at these sentences. Notice how the descriptive word is used.

El loro es **verde**.

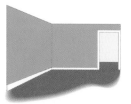

La pared es **verde**.

Did you see that the descriptive word is the same in both cases? Descriptive words that don't end in **-o** or **-a** stay the same for words that use **el** *and* words that use **la.**

Now, here are some words you can use to talk about sizes and shapes:

grande

pequeño

|← **largo** →| →|**corto**|←

If you want to ask for a description of something, ask **¿Cómo es?**

—**¿Cómo es el oso?**
—**Es grande.**

A. Josefina is talking about the colors of different animals and objects. Help her complete each sentence.

El bolígrafo es (rosado, rosada).
El bolígrafo es rosado.

1. La mariposa es (rojo, roja).

2. La pared es (blanco, blanca).

3. El tigre es (anaranjado, anaranjada).

4. El oso es (negro, negra).

5. La regla es (morado, morada).

6. El mapa es (amarillo, amarilla).

B. You and a friend are looking at some magazines. Your friend wants to test your knowledge of colors as you both look at the pictures.

PARTNER A: Ask what color the animal or object is.
PARTNER B: Say what the color is.

—¿De qué color es el perro?
—Es blanco.

1.
2.
3.
4.

5.
6.
7.
8.

C. How would you describe different objects in your classroom? Look around you, then answer the questions.

—¿Es grande o pequeño el bolígrafo?
—**El bolígrafo es grande.**

1. ¿Es larga o corta la tiza?

2. ¿Es grande o pequeño un cuaderno?

3. ¿Es largo o corto el escritorio?

4. ¿Es larga o corta una regla?

5. ¿Es grande o pequeña una silla?

6. ¿Es grande o pequeño el mapa?

ENTRE AMIGOS

 Bring in a picture of your favorite animal. It can be a photo, a drawing, or an illustration in a book. Be prepared to answer questions and talk about your animal.

Sit in groups of three or four. Show your picture. The people in your group will ask you different questions. After they're done, you can add any information they might have missed.

Look at the questions Amanda's group asked her:

—**Amanda, ¿cuál es tu animal favorito?**

—**Es un pez.**

—**¿Cómo se llama tu pez?**
—**Se llama Goldie.**

—**¿De qué color es?**
—**Es anaranjado.**

—**¿Cómo es Goldie?**
—**Es pequeño.**

Here are the names of some other animals:

horse:	**el caballo**	cow:	**la vaca**
duck:	**el pato**	hen:	**la gallina**
lion:	**el león**	rooster:	**el gallo**
giraffe:	**la jirafa**	snake:	**la culebra**
donkey:	**el burro**	elephant:	**el elefante**

¿Cómo lo dices?

Describing more than one

Look at these sentences. Notice how the words that describe the animals change when we talk about more than one.

El os**o** es negr**o**.

Los os**os** son negr**os**.

La maripos**a** es amarill**a**.

Las maripos**as** son amarill**as**.

El perr**o** es grand**e**.

Los perr**os** son grand**es**.

If the descriptive word ends in a vowel, then add an **-s** when you talk about more than one. Some descriptive words—for example, **azul**—don't end in a vowel. Add **-es** to these words to talk about more than one.

A. Mariela is talking about her favorite animals and other things. Help her complete each sentence with the correct word.

El lápiz es (marrón, marrones).
El lápiz es marrón

1.  La silla es (morada, moradas).

2.  Los conejos son (gris, grises).

3.  Los canarios son (amarillo, amarillos).

4.  Las mariposas son (azul, azules).

5.  El oso es (negro, negros).

Este pájaro es un tucán.

B. Help Alberto complete some sentences he wants to write. Write the sentences on a separate piece of paper. Use colors or other words to describe the pictures.

El ratón es _____.
El ratón es pequeño.

1.   Los perros son _____.

2.    La bandera es _____.

3.    El pupitre es _____.

4.    Las reglas son _____.

5.    La pared es _____.

¿Cómo lo dices?

Talking about things in general

So far you've learned how to use **el** and **la**, as well as **un** and **una**. Do you know when to use one and when to use the other? Look at these examples.

Es **un** gato.

El gato es gris.

Es **una** regla.

La regla es larga.

You use **un** or **una** to talk about something in general, and **el** or **la** to talk about one specific thing. The English words *a, an* and *the* work the same way.

Now look at what happens to **un** and **una** when you're talking about more than one thing.

un pez

unos peces

una pared

unas paredes

Un changes to **unos** and **una** changes to **unas**.

A. Play a guessing game with a partner.

PARTNER A: Read the question.
PARTNER B: Look at the picture and answer the question.

—¿Es un pájaro?
—**No, no es un pájaro. Es un perro.**

1. ¿Son unos perros?

2. ¿Es una mariposa?

3. ¿Son unos canarios?

4. ¿Es un ratón?

¿Cómo son los leones marinos?

B. You are a contestant on a game show and your partner is the game show host. If you answer all the questions correctly, you will win the grand prize!

PARTNER A: Look at the picture and ask the questions.

PARTNER B: Answer based on the picture.

—¿Qué es esto?
—Es un oso.
—¿Cómo es el oso?
—Es grande.

1. ¿Qué es esto?
¿De qué color es _____?

2. ¿Qué son estos?
¿De qué color son _____?

3. ¿Qué es esto?
¿Cómo es _____?

4. ¿Qué son estas?
¿De qué color son _____?

5. ¿Qué es esto?
¿Cómo es _____?

6. ¿Qué son estos?
¿Cómo son _____?

ENTRE AMIGOS

 Together with three or four of your classmates, write the names of all the animals you learned about in this unit on separate pieces of paper. Then put them in a small bag.

Pick out one of the papers and imitate the animal named on it. Your classmates will guess the animal (in Spanish, of course), and add a sentence describing the animal. The first person to guess correctly wins a point. So does the first person who describes the animal! Take turns and play to eight points.

Es un oso.

El oso es blanco.

¡El oso es grande!

To liven up the game, add Spanish sound effects to your acting.

guau, guau   **miau, miau**   **cua, cua**   **i-o, i-o**

En una escuela en Colombia

En un parque en Madrid, España

En casa el fin de semana

¿Sabes que...?

In Spanish-speaking countries:

● School days tend to be longer since kids usually have more subjects— sometimes up to ten a day!

● When you go to a park, you can almost always find people playing *fútbol*—soccer.

● People often celebrate their birthdays in the park.

● Kids love to go places. Stores and theaters are among their favorites.

What are the days of the week?

—¿Cuáles son los días de la semana?

—Lunes, martes, miércoles, jueves, viernes, sábado y domingo.

—¿Y del fin de semana?

—Sábado y domingo.

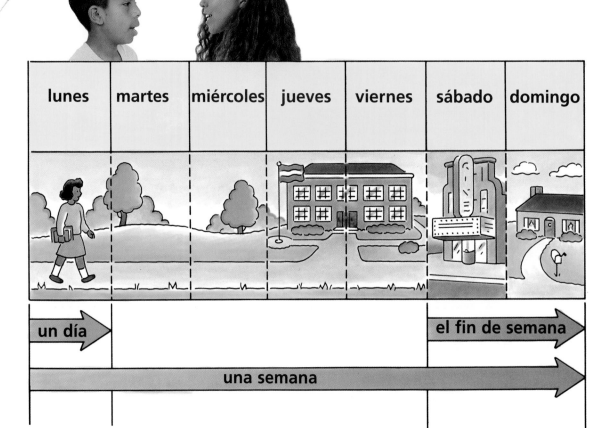

lunes	martes	miércoles	jueves	viernes	sábado	domingo

un día

el fin de semana

una semana

—¿Qué día es hoy? ¿Lunes?

—Sí, y mañana es martes, ¡claro!

hoy

el calendario

lunes	martes	miércoles	jueves	viernes	sábado	domingo
	1̶ el primero	2̶	3̶	4̶	5̶	6̶
⑦	8 mañana	9	10	11	12	13
14	15	16				
28	29	30 el treinta	31 el treinta y uno			

—¿Qué día es el primero?

—Es el martes.

PRACTIQUEMOS

A. Your friends are making plans. They need to know the days for certain dates. Work with a partner.

PARTNER **A:**   Ask what day of the week a certain date is.

PARTNER **B:**   Look at the calendar and answer.

—¿Qué día es el tres?

—**Es el domingo.**

1. ¿Qué día es el seis?

2. ¿Qué día es el veintidós?

3. ¿Qué día es el veinticinco?

4. ¿Qué día es el cinco?

5. ¿Qué día es el diecisiete?

6. ¿Qué día es el primero?

7. ¿Qué día es el veintiocho?

8. ¿Qué día es el trece?

9. ¿Qué día es el once?

10. ¿Qué día es el veintiuno?

lunes	martes	miércoles	jueves	viernes	sábado	domingo
				1	2	3
4	5	6	7	8	9	10
11	12	13	14	15	16	17
18	19	20	21	22	23	24
25	26	27	28	29	30	

B. With a partner, make up a calendar for the first two weeks of next month. Write the name for each date in Spanish. Trade calendars with another pair of classmates and check each other's work.

ENTRE AMIGOS

For this game, you'll need a chalkboard or large "scoreboard," and a tennis ball or other lightweight ball.

Choose a scorekeeper. Then form two teams. A player from Team A starts by saying a day of the week, and throws the ball to any player from Team B. That player must name the day that follows:

TEAM A PLAYER:	Sábado.
TEAM B PLAYER:	Domingo.

If the player answers correctly, then Team B scores a point. Then that same player says a new day of the week, and throws the ball to any player from Team A. (You may wish to change the rules after a while, and name the day before.)

The team that scores the most points wins.

Sábado en Lima, Perú

¡HABLEMOS!

Where are you going?

—¿Adónde vas el lunes?
—Voy a la escuela.

la escuela

la casa
Es la casa de Iris.

la tienda

Voy al mercado.

¡FÍJATE!

¡Fíjate! means "Pay attention!" or "Watch out!" When you see this, you'll find information about things to keep in mind.

El lunes means "this Monday." *Los lunes* means "on Mondays" or "every Monday."

lunes	martes	miércoles	jueves	viernes	sábado	domingo
	X	X	X	X	X	X
7 hoy	8	9	esta semana		12	13
14	15	16	la próxima semana		19	20
21	22	23	24	25	26	27
28	29	30				

—¿Cuándo vas al cine?

—Voy el domingo. OR Voy esta semana.

el cine

el parque

¿Cuándo vas al parque?

Vamos a la escuela.

PRACTIQUEMOS

A. **¿Adónde vas?** Answer using the words and pictures.

Voy al parque.

Voy al _____.

1. Voy a la _____.

2. Voy al _____.

3. Voy a la _____.

4. Voy a la _____.

B. You're talking to different friends who are telling you where they are going. You want to know when.

PARTNER A: Ask when your friend is going to the place indicated.

PARTNER B: Answer based on the information.

al cine / la próxima semana   —**¿Cuándo vas al cine?**
—**Voy la próxima semana.**

1. a la escuela / el lunes   **3.** al parque / esta semana

2. a la tienda / el miércoles   **4.** a la casa de Corina / hoy

ENTRE AMIGOS

 See if you and your friends have similar schedules. Make a chart like this:

¿Cuándo vas ...	¿Hoy?	¿Mañana?	¿Esta semana?	¿La próxima semana?
al cine?	✓			
a la tienda?				✓
al parque?				
a la escuela?	✓	✓	✓	✓
a la casa?	✓	✓	✓	✓

Put a check in each box that applies to you. Then get together with four or five classmates. Ask them the questions to see if they have similar schedules planned:

¿Cuándo vas al cine?

¿Hoy?

¿Mañana?

¿Esta semana?

¿La próxima semana?

¿Cómo lo dices?

Talking about going places

Look at the pictures. What words tell where the people are going?

Voy **a la** escuela.

Voy **al** parque.

Voy **al** cine.

Voy **al** salón de clase.

Voy **a la** tienda.

Voy **a la** casa de José.

Did you notice that some sentences have **al** and some sentences have **a la?**

In Spanish, when you talk about going to places, use **al** with **el** words:

el parque ⟶ **Voy al parque.**

For words with **la,** use **a la:**

la tienda ⟶ **Voy a la tienda.**

¡Úsalo!

A. Talk about where you're going. Work with a partner.

PARTNER A: Ask if your friend is going to the place in picture "a."

PARTNER B: Say no, you are going to the place in picture "b."

—¿Vas al parque?
—No, voy a la escuela.

a.   b.

1. a.    b.

2. a.    b.

3. a.    b.

4. a.    b.

ENTRE AMIGOS

Do you like to make schedules? Sometimes they're important.

On a separate piece of paper, write the days and dates for the next seven days. Your chart might look like this:

lunes	martes	miércoles	jueves	viernes	sábado	domingo
21	**22**	**23**	**24**	**25**	**26**	**27**

Under each date, write the name of a place you're going to that day. For example, under **"domingo–27,"** you might write: **"el parque."**

Now get together with a partner. Take turns asking and answering questions. Your partner asks you a question like:

¿Adónde vas el domingo?

You might answer: **Voy al parque.**

Or your partner might ask: **¿Cuándo vas al parque?**

You might answer: **Voy el veintisiete.** OR **Voy el domingo.**

¿CÓMO LO DICES?

Who's going?

In each set of sentences, what words are different?

Voy a la escuela.   **Vas** a la escuela.   **Va** a la escuela.

Voy al cine.   **¿Vas** al cine?   **Va** al cine.

In each picture, the *person* who is going changes. Use **voy** to talk about yourself, **vas** to talk to your brothers, sisters, and other kids, and **va** to talk to or about another person. **Voy, vas,** and **va** all come from the verb **ir,** which means "to go."

 A. Your little brother is confused about where you're going on different days. Help him out.

PARTNER A: Ask the question.
PARTNER B: Answer according to the picture.

 —¿Vas al parque hoy?
—**No, no voy al parque. Voy a la casa.**

1. ¿Vas al cine el lunes?

2. ¿Vas a la casa de Julio el domingo?

3. ¿Vas a la tienda el viernes?

4. ¿Vas a la escuela el sábado?

B. Now your brother wants to know where your friends are going on certain days. You just happen to have a calendar of their activities:

	Elena	Jaime	María	Jorge
lunes	la casa	la escuela	la escuela	la escuela
martes	la escuela	la escuela	la escuela	la escuela
miércoles	la escuela	el parque	la escuela	la tienda
jueves	el parque	la escuela	la escuela	la escuela
viernes	la tienda	el parque	la tienda	el cine
sábado	la casa	la escuela	el cine	el parque
domingo	el cine	la casa	el parque	la casa

PARTNER A: Ask the question.

PARTNER B: Answer according to the schedule.

—¿Va Elena a la escuela el lunes?

—**No, no va a la escuela. Va a la casa.**

1. ¿Va Jaime al cine el sábado? no

2. ¿Va María a la casa el martes? no

3. ¿Va Jorge a la tienda el viernes? no

4. ¿Va Elena al parque el viernes? no

5. ¿Va Jorge al cine el lunes?

6. ¿Va Jaime a la tienda el domingo?

ENTRE AMIGOS

 Here's a memory game. Form a circle with four other classmates.

One person starts by asking the next player **¿Adónde vas?** The player responds. For example, **Voy al cine.**

Then the first player asks, **¿Cuándo vas al cine?** The player responds **Voy** (**hoy, esta semana, la próxima semana, el lunes, el fin de semana,** etc.). Go around the circle until everyone has had a chance to ask and answer the two questions.

Now everyone in the group should take out a piece of paper and write down where the other people are going, and when:

Jorge va a la tienda la próxima semana. Carmen va...

Compare sentences to see whose memory is the best!

Tiendas en México

¡A divertirnos!

Make a town from shoeboxes or other cardboard boxes. Create **un cine, tiendas, escuelas,** and **casas.** Leave an open area for **el parque.** Give each place a name and street number.

Make small figures out of cardboard or other material. Give them names. Make up schedules of activities for them, and move them around the town.

En la escuela

**What does your class schedule look like?
Do you have many different classes? What
about classes like music and art?**

If your schedule is full and busy, you probably talk with your
classmates about what you're going to do next.

In this unit, you'll learn to:

- Talk about classes you go to

- Talk about other places in your school

- Talk about what you're going to do

- Talk about school activities

- Learn about school activities in Spanish-speaking countries

¿Sabes usar la
computadora?

Una clase de música en Miami

¡HABLEMOS!

Where are you going?

—¿Adónde vas?

—Voy al gimnasio.

el gimnasio

la clase de computadoras

¿Adónde vas?

la clase de música

la clase de arte

la biblioteca

Voy a...

¿Es la biblioteca
o es la clase de
arte?

PRACTIQUEMOS

Your friends keep leaving the room. Ask them where they're going.

PARTNER A: Ask where the person is going.
PARTNER B: Answer according to the picture.

—¿Adónde vas?
—Voy a la clase de música.

1.

2.

3.

4.

Arte en la calle

ENTRE AMIGOS

 Francisco has made some notes to himself about where he'll be on three different days this week:

lunes
la escuela
la clase de música
la biblioteca

miércoles
la escuela
el gimnasio
la clase de arte
la tienda

viernes
la escuela
el gimnasio
la clase de computadoras
el cine

Where are *you* going this week? Write some reminder notes to yourself for three days of this week. Write at least two places for each note.

Pair up with someone and exchange notes. See if you and your partner can remember your notes without looking back at what you wrote.

Ask each other questions like these:

¿Adónde vas el lunes?

¿Cuándo vas a la clase de arte?

¿Vas al gimnasio el viernes?

¿Vas a la tienda el lunes?

¿Vas a la clase de música esta semana?

¡HABLEMOS!

What are you going to do?

—¿Qué vas a hacer?

—Voy a pintar.

pintar

estudiar

cantar

practicar los
deportes

usar la
computadora

Deportes en un
colegio de España

PRACTIQUEMOS

Your young neighbor hasn't started school yet and is very curious about what you do in school.

PARTNER A: Ask what your partner is going to do in the class or place indicated by the picture.

PARTNER B: Answer according to the picture.

—¿Qué vas a hacer en la clase de arte?
—Voy a pintar.

la clase de arte

1. la biblioteca

2. la clase de computadoras

3. la clase de música

4. el gimnasio

ENTRE AMIGOS

How well do your friends know you?

Make a list of the five school activities you just learned. List the activity you most enjoy first, and give it 5 points. Then list your next favorite, and give it 4 points, and so on. Here's an example:

cantar – 5
pintar – 4
usar la computadora – 3
practicar los deportes – 2
estudiar – 1

Now ask a partner **¿Qué voy a hacer?**

Your partner will answer **Vas a...** three times, each time naming an activity from the list of five choices. When your partner completes his or her answers, add up the point values of the activities that were chosen. Then change roles with your partner and *you* answer the question. When you finish, compare point totals. Which of you knows the other better?

¿Practicas deportes?

¿CÓMO LO DICES?

What are you going to do?

Here's how you say you're going to do something:

Voy a pintar.

¿Vas a pintar?

Va a pintar.

Voy a estudiar.

¿Vas a estudiar?

Va a estudiar.

To say that someone is going to do something, you use **voy a, vas a,** or **va a** plus another verb that tells *what* the person is going to do.

¡ÚSALO!

A. Andrea wants to know what all her classmates are going to do tomorrow. Answer her questions about people's activities.

> (practicar los deportes)   —¿Qué va a hacer Miguel?
> —**Miguel va a practicar los deportes.**

1. ¿Qué va a hacer José?
   (estudiar)

2. ¿Qué va a hacer Carlos?
   (usar la computadora)

3. ¿Qué va a hacer Amalia?
   (ir a la tienda)

4. ¿Qué va a hacer Alba?
   (pintar en el salón de clase)

5. ¿Qué va a hacer Sonia?
   (cantar)

6. ¿Qué va a hacer Felipe?
   (ir a la clase de arte)

B. Rogelio is asking his friends what they're doing tomorrow.

| PARTNER **A:** | Read the question. |
| PARTNER **B:** | Look at the face, then answer. |

> —¿Vas a cantar mañana?
> —**No, no voy a cantar mañana.**

1. ¿Vas a ir al cine mañana?

2. ¿Vas a practicar los deportes mañana?

3. ¿Vas a pintar mañana?

4. ¿Vas a usar la computadora mañana?

5. ¿Vas a estudiar mañana?

6. ¿Vas a ir al gimnasio mañana?

ENTRE AMIGOS

 Make some plans with classmates to do something or go somewhere today, tomorrow, this week, or next week.

Get in a group of three classmates. One person starts by asking one of the other students what he or she is going to do:

¿Qué vas a hacer mañana, Alicia?

The other person answers:

Voy a (estudiar en la biblioteca).

Then the third person in your group tells you what this person is going to do:

Alicia va a estudiar en la biblioteca.

Now another person asks the question and the other two respond. Each time you ask a question, use a new day or week, and keep changing the activities you're going to do. See how fast you can do the activity!

Esta famosa biblioteca está en México.

¿Cómo lo dices?

What do you do in your classes?

Here's how you can use words like **pintar, estudiar,** and **cantar** to tell what people do.

Pint**o** muy bien.

Pint**as** muy bien.

Pint**a** muy bien.

Estudi**o** mucho.

Estudi**as** mucho.

Luis estudi**a** mucho.

Cant**o** en la clase.

Cant**as** en la clase.

Iris cant**a** en la clase.

Action words have different endings to show who is doing the action. With verbs that end in **-ar,** use the **-o** ending to talk about yourself, the **-as** ending to talk to a friend, and the **-a** ending to talk about another person.

You can also talk about *how* a person does something. If the person does something *well,* you can say

Pinta muy bien.

If the person does something *a lot,* you can say

Estudia mucho.

A. You're showing your neighbor some photos of friends at school. As you look at each picture, say the person's name and what that person does.

Marta

Marta practica los deportes.

1. Ramón

2. Jorge

3. Victoria

4. Bárbara

B. What are your friends doing around the school? Read each item and give your answer, like this:

Marta / pintar / la clase de arte
Marta pinta en la clase de arte.

1. Ricardo / cantar / la clase de música

2. Tomás / pintar / la clase de arte

3. Ana / estudiar / la biblioteca

4. Clara / practicar los deportes / el gimnasio

5. José / usar la computadora / la clase de computadoras

C. One of your neighbors is asking you about your activities in and around school. Answer his questions.

PARTNER A: Ask the question.
PARTNER B: Answer the questions honestly.

—¿Practicas mucho los deportes?
—Sí, practico mucho los deportes.

1. ¿Estudias mucho los sábados?

2. ¿Pintas muy bien?

3. ¿Practicas los deportes en el gimnasio?

4. ¿Cantas en la clase de música?

5. ¿Usas la computadora en la escuela?

6. ¿Pintas mucho en la casa?

D. Look at these school activities. For each one, think of one classmate who does the activity a lot, and another classmate who doesn't. Write sentences like those shown:

estudiar   pintar   cantar
   usar la computadora   practicar los deportes

practicar los deportes   **Carlos practica los deportes mucho. Analía no practica los deportes mucho.**

Are you right about your classmates? To find out, ask them.

—**Carlos, ¿practicas los deportes mucho?**
—**Sí, practico los deportes mucho.** OR **No, no practico los deportes mucho.**

ENTRE AMIGOS

Write an article for a class newspaper. Interview a classmate. Ask at least three questions about his or her activities, then write a paragraph. Here's an example:

Raúl pinta mucho. Pinta en la clase de arte. En la escuela, pinta el lunes, el martes, el jueves y el viernes. No pinta el miércoles. En la casa pinta el fin de semana.

Exchange papers with a classmate. Read your classmate's paragraph and give ideas for any changes. Make the changes before you submit your paragraph to the newspaper editor (your teacher).

¡A divertirnos!

This is a game called "Find Someone Who...." Make a list of five sentences about activities, but leave a blank for the name of the person who does each activity. Here are some examples:

1. _____ **pinta mucho.**

2. _____ **practica los deportes en el gimnasio.**

3. _____ **usa la computadora muy bien.**

4. _____ **estudia mucho.**

5. _____ **canta muy bien.**

Now walk around and ask different people in the class if they do a certain activity. You might ask:

María, ¿pintas mucho?

If the person's answer is **Sí,** or **Sí, pinto mucho**, write the person's name in the correct blank:

1. María pinta mucho.

Keep asking and answering until all your blanks are filled. Remember, other classmates will be asking you questions, as well. The first pair to get all blanks filled is the winner.

¿Cuál estación te gusta?

What is the weather like where you live? Does it get very hot in the summer? Does it rain a lot in the spring?

What do you like to do when the weather changes? Maybe you like to do outdoor activities as much as possible—even in the winter.

In this unit, you're going to:

- Learn about the seasons
- Talk about different kinds of weather
- Talk about what you like—and don't like
- Use descriptive words to name the things you like
- Learn about the weather and seasons in Spanish-speaking countries

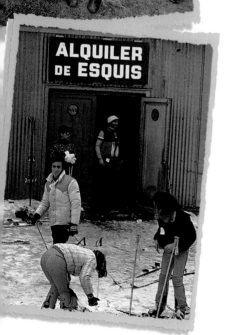

La primavera en Córdoba, España es muy linda.

Está lloviendo en Colombia.

¿Sabes que...?

- Not all Spanish-speaking countries have hot weather all year long. Some can get as cold as Alaska.

- Christmas is a popular time to go to the beach in Argentina. It's usually around 100° Fahrenheit.

- The climate in Perú varies greatly, from steaming, hot jungles to snowy mountaintops that are always frozen.

Nieva en España.

¡HABLEMOS!

What season do you like?

—¿Cuál estación te gusta?

—Me gusta el verano.

el verano

el otoño

el invierno

la primavera

—¿Qué tiempo hace?
—Hace fresco.

Hace fresco.

Hace calor.

Nieva.

Hace frío.

Hace sol.

Llueve.

Así es... As you know, the equator *(el ecuador)* divides the world into the Northern Hemisphere and the Southern Hemisphere. Places close to the equator have similar seasons. But the differences become greater as you get farther from the equator. For example, it is summer in Chile and Argentina when it is winter in the U. S. And when the U.S. is enjoying warm summer days, Chile and Argentina are in the middle of their winter.

PRACTIQUEMOS

A. Each of these pictures was taken during a different season. For each one, answer the question **¿Cuál es la estación?**

1.   2.   3.   4.

 B. You're talking to a group of exchange students from all over the world, asking them questions about the weather in their countries.

PARTNER A: Ask the question about the weather.
PARTNER B: Answer according to the picture.

—¿Qué tiempo hace en el invierno?
—Nieva.

1. ¿Qué tiempo hace en el otoño? 2. ¿Qué tiempo hace en el verano? 3. ¿Qué tiempo hace en el invierno?

4. ¿Qué tiempo hace en la primavera?

5. ¿Qué tiempo hace en el invierno?

 C. Your little brother is learning about seasons and weather in school. Answer his questions.

PARTNER A: Ask the question about the weather.
PARTNER B: Answer according to the weather where you live.

—¿Hace calor en el invierno?
—**No, no hace calor en el invierno.**

1. ¿Llueve en el verano?

2. ¿Hace calor en la primavera?

3. ¿Hace frío en el invierno?

4. ¿Nieva en el verano?

5. ¿Hace fresco en el otoño?

6. ¿Hace sol en el invierno?

7. ¿Hace fresco en la primavera?

8. ¿Cuándo hace sol?

¿Qué tiempo hace?

¡HABLEMOS!

What's the weather like now?

—¿Qué tiempo hace ahora?
—Hace buen tiempo.

Hace buen tiempo.

Hace mal tiempo.

Está nublado.

Hace viento.

Está lloviendo.

Está nevando.

Así es...

A very interesting weather event occurs off the western coast of South America every 4 to 12 years. It is called *El niño*, which means "the child." As a result of *El niño*, the surface of the ocean warms. It causes plankton and fish to die and affects weather over much of the Pacific Ocean. Sometimes it even causes terrible hurricanes. Why do you think it's called *El niño*?

PRACTIQUEMOS

A. What a crazy day! Your friend keeps asking you about the weather, and each time you look out the window, it's different!

PARTNER A: Ask the question about the weather.
PARTNER B: Answer according to the picture.

—¿Hace buen tiempo ahora?
—No, hace viento ahora.

1. ¿Hace mal tiempo ahora?

2. ¿Está nublado ahora?

3. ¿Hace viento ahora?

4. ¿Está lloviendo ahora?

5. ¿Está nevando ahora?

6. ¿Hace buen tiempo ahora?

B. As part of a science project, you have to fill out a questionnaire about the weather where you live. Use your notebook to write the answers to the questions.

1. ¿Hace buen tiempo en la primavera?

2. ¿Hace viento en el verano?

3. ¿Hace calor en el verano?

4. ¿Nieva en el invierno?

5. ¿Hace fresco en el otoño?

6. ¿Llueve en la primavera?

7. ¿Hace mal tiempo en el otoño?

8. ¿Qué tiempo hace ahora?

¿Qué tiempo hace en Costa Rica hoy?

Una tormenta en el océano

¿CÓMO LO DICES?

Talking about likes and dislikes

How do you talk about liking something? Look at these sentences to learn how.

Me gusta pintar.

¿Te gusta pintar?

A Juan le gusta pintar.

Me gusta el verano.

¿Te gusta el verano?

A Delia le gusta
el verano.

Did you notice that the ending is the same (**gusta**) in all the sentences? In each sentence, how do you know *who* likes something?

The words **me, te,** and **le** give you that information. You use **me gusta** to talk about yourself, **te gusta** to talk to a friend, and **le gusta** to talk about someone else.

Talking about dislikes works the same way:

No me gusta cantar.   **¿No te gusta** pintar?   **A Víctor no le gusta** el invierno.

Look back at the different sentences in this section. What's different about the sentences with the names Juan, Delia, and Víctor?

A. Andrés is a new student in class. Look at the faces, then answer his questions about some of his new classmates.

—¿A Gilberto le gusta estudiar?
—**No, a Gilberto no le gusta estudiar.**

 1. ¿A Clara le gusta pintar?

2. ¿A Mateo le gusta ir a la biblioteca?

3. ¿A Lupe le gusta practicar los deportes?

4. ¿A Paula le gusta usar la computadora?

B. You're with a new friend who wants to know what you really like or don't like.

PARTNER A: Ask the question.
PARTNER B: Answer according to your likes and dislikes.

—¿Te gusta el invierno?
—**Sí, me gusta el invierno.**

1. ¿Te gusta estudiar?

2. ¿Te gusta la primavera?

3. ¿Te gusta la clase de arte?

4. ¿Te gusta el verano?

5. ¿Te gusta ir a la escuela?

6. ¿Te gusta ir al cine?

ENTRE AMIGOS

 Take a survey of your classmates. Choose a question from the list and ask ten people to answer it. Record the answers. Afterwards, compare surveys with others.

Preguntas

1. ¿Cuál estación te gusta mucho?
2. ¿Qué te gusta hacer los sábados?
3. ¿Qué te gusta hacer en la casa?

4. ¿Te gusta ir al cine?
5. ¿Te gusta practicar los deportes?

Which one do you like?

When we use a descriptive word in English, it comes before the word it describes: *the **blue** house, the **big** bird.* But look where the descriptive words are in Spanish:

No me gusta **el perro grande.**

Me gusta **el triángulo verde.**

Do they come before or after the word they describe?

When we're describing things in English, we don't always say the name of the thing we're describing: *I like the blue **one.** Do you have the big **one?*** Here is how you do that in Spanish:

—¿Cuál te gusta, el bolígrafo rojo o el bolígrafo amarillo?

—Me gusta **el amarillo.**

—¿Cuál te gusta, la bandera azul o la bandera verde?

—Me gusta **la verde.**

—¿Cuál perro te gusta?

—Me gusta **el marrón.**

Do you see that you just use **el** or **la** and the descriptive word?

¡ÚSALO!

A. You are in charge of decorating the bulletin board with pictures. Read the question and choose the indicated picture.

—¿Cuál te gusta, el gato gris o el gato marrón?
—Me gusta el marrón.

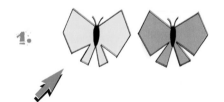

1. ¿Cuál te gusta, la mariposa amarilla o la mariposa azul?

2. ¿Cuál te gusta, el tigre grande o el tigre pequeño?

3.  ¿Cuál te gusta, el pájaro azul o el pájaro rojo?

4. 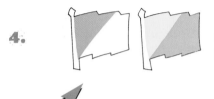 ¿Cuál te gusta, la bandera verde y blanca o la bandera amarilla y azul?

¿Qué bandera te gusta?

B. You and a friend are in a pet shop talking about the animals.

PARTNER A: Say what animals are for sale.
PARTNER B: Ask which one your partner likes.

—**Hay un gato anaranjado y un gato negro.**
—**¿Cuál te gusta, el anaranjado o el negro?**

1.

2.

3.

4.

Proverbio: A mal tiempo, buena cara.

Entre Amigos

 Play a game. Cut out squares of different colors—all the colors you've learned so far in Spanish.

Go up to five different classmates. Without looking, pick two of your squares, hold them up, and ask your classmate **¿Cuál te gusta?** Your classmate responds **Me gusta (el verde).** Give your classmate the one he or she likes. Then your classmate asks the question. You answer and your classmate gives you a color square.

Now put your color squares on your desk. Your teacher will name a color—for example: **el azul.** Stand up if you have that color. Your teacher will name more colors. Sit down if you don't have the color named. If you do have that color, you should remain standing. Which colors are the most popular?

¡A divertirnos!

Look at these two charts of average temperatures. The top chart is for places north of the equator. The bottom one is for places south of the equator. Notice that the temperatures are given in two ways—in degrees Fahrenheit and in degrees Celsius. (If you hear a weather report in South America, the forecaster will say something like **La temperatura en Caracas es de veinte grados Celsius.** [The temperature in Caracas is twenty degrees Celsius.] They don't give temperatures in **grados Fahrenheit.**)

Las temperaturas al norte del ecuador

	Invierno	Verano
Bogotá, Colombia	57°F/14°C	58°F/14°C
Caracas, Venezuela	66°F/19°C	70°F/21°C
Dallas, Estados Unidos	45°F/7°C	86°F/30°C
Montreal, Canadá	22°F/-6°C	79°F/26°C
Tegucigalpa, Honduras	50°F/10°C	90°F/32°C

Las temperaturas al sur del ecuador

	Verano	Invierno
Buenos Aires, Argentina	74°F/23°C	52°F/11°C
Lima, Perú	77°F/25°C	59°F/15°C
La Paz, Bolivia	53°F/12°C	48°F/9°C
Montevideo, Uruguay	72°F/22°C	55°F/13°C
Tierra del Fuego, Argentina	50°F/10°C	32°F/0°C

Now get in a group of five classmates. Take turns playing forecaster. Choose one of the cities on the chart. Announce the day of the week and the season, and give the temperature for that day. Add other information about the weather, if you wish.

UNIDAD 6

¡Siempre patino en julio!

You probably don't go skating in July like a lot of kids in Chile do. But do you go swimming?

What other things do you do in July? Each month you do different things, from swimming and skating to celebrating birthdays (**cumpleaños**) and holidays (**días de fiesta**).

In this unit, you're going to:

- Learn the months of the year
- Talk about the things you like to do in different months
- Talk about who's doing something
- Tell people dates (like your birthday!)
- Talk about how often you do things
- Learn about holidays in Spanish-speaking countries

¡Un día de fiesta!

Ciclismo en España

¿Sabes que...?

● The most popular sport in Spanish-speaking countries is soccer *(fútbol).* It's played all year long.

● *Piñatas* are popular at birthday parties in Latin America. They are made of papier mâché and are full of fruit, candy, and other treats. Kids take turns trying to break them open with a stick.

● Every July 7th in Pamplona, Spain, people let wild bulls run through the streets of the city to celebrate the Feast of San Fermín.

Esquiando en los Andes en junio

¡Hablemos!

What's the date?

—¿Cuál es la fecha?

—Es el trece de enero.

13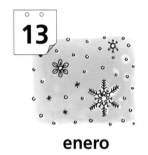

enero

14

febrero

17

marzo

8

abril

5

mayo

21

junio

4

julio

27

agosto

15

septiembre

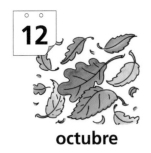
octubre

noviembre

diciembre

—¿En qué mes es tu cumpleaños?

—En noviembre. Es el doce de noviembre.

¡Es mi cumpleaños!

PRACTIQUEMOS

A. How good is your memory? Look at each picture and tell what month it is.

Es abril.

1. 2. 3. 4.

5. 6. 7. 8.

B. **¿Cuál es la fecha?** Now that you've learned the months, you're able to give dates in Spanish. Give the dates for each of these holidays.

1. 2. 3.

4.   5.   6.

ENTRE AMIGOS

 Most people like to be wished a happy birthday. Your class is going to make a birthday list so you'll know everyone's birthday.

Pick a partner and ask the date of his or her birthday—in Spanish, of course! Your partner will answer, and then ask your birth date. Your teacher will write the names of the months on a list, and call out the names of each month. When your partner's birthday month is called, raise your hand and tell your partner's name and birthday.

El cumpleaños de Marcos es el primero de octubre.

Your teacher will put the list in a place where everyone can see it. Check the list every day to see if someone has a birthday. Be sure to wish them…

¡FELIZ CUMPLEAÑOS!

¡Hablemos!

What do you like to do?

—¿Qué te gusta hacer los fines de semana?
—Me gusta nadar.
—Me gusta nadar también.

nadar

bailar

caminar

patinar

Ellos bailan para celebrar un día de fiesta en el Perú.

Así es...

For many people in Spanish-speaking countries, a person's "saint's day" *(santo)* is celebrated in addition to, or in place of, his or her actual birthday. Each day of the year is named for a saint. The day with your name is your "saint's day." This way, you have two special days to celebrate each year!

PRACTIQUEMOS

 A. You and a new friend from Spain are talking about what you like to do.

PARTNER A: Ask the question based on the picture.
PARTNER B: Answer according to the word in parentheses.

¿Te gusta  ? (no)

—**¿Te gusta pintar?**
—**No, no me gusta pintar.**

1. ¿Te gusta  ? (sí)

2. ¿Te gusta  ? (no)

3. ¿Te gusta  ? (no)

4. ¿Te gusta  ? (sí)

5. ¿Te gusta  ? (no)

6. ¿Te gusta ? (no)

B. You're sitting in a park with one of your friends. You're comparing what you both like to do during different months.

PARTNER **A:** Ask what your friend likes to do during a certain month.

PARTNER **B:** Respond according to what you think.

PARTNER **A:** Agree or disagree.

—¿Qué te gusta hacer en abril?
—En abril me gusta caminar.
—Me gusta caminar en abril también. OR
No me gusta caminar en abril. Me gusta nadar.

Ask each other about three different months.

ENTRE AMIGOS

Work with a partner and make up your own magazine cover. First pick a name for your magazine, then choose a month and date for publishing your special magazine issue.

Use a separate piece of paper to make up your cover. Cut out or draw a picture of a famous person and glue it to your cover. Under the picture, write what your famous personality likes to do.

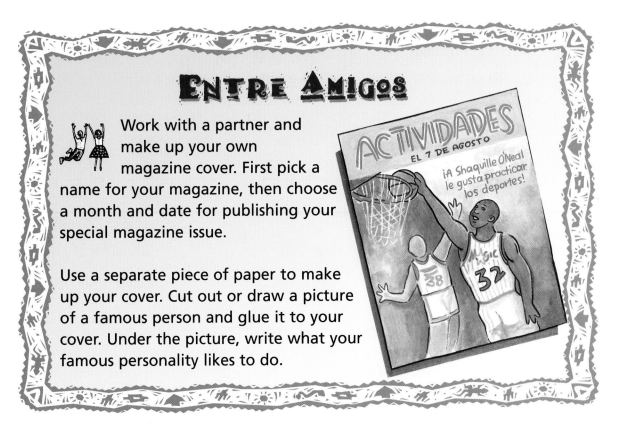

¿Cómo lo dices?

Who's doing what?

Study the sentence with each picture. Which word tells you who is painting?

¿Quién pinta?

Yo pinto.

Tú pintas.

Él pinta.

Ella pinta.

Usted pinta.

In English, to say who is doing something, you can use the person's name or you can substitute a word like *I, you, he,* or *she.* You can do the same thing in Spanish with the words **yo, tú, él, ella**, and **usted.**

But many times, people who speak Spanish leave these words out.

—¿Nadas mucho?

—Sí. Nado los sábados y los domingos.

You only need the name or word to make sure people know whom you're talking about.

—¿Quién nada, tú o Juan?

—*Yo* nado.

A. Speak up! Look at the pictures and tell your teacher and classmates what you do.

Yo nado.

1.

2.

3.

4.

B. Ask a friend if he or she does the activities in the pictures.

—¿Bailas tú?
—Sí, yo bailo. OR No, yo no bailo.

1.

2.

3.

C. Try Exercise B again, but this time, ask your teacher!

—¿Baila usted?

D. Your friend is organizing a school festival, but he doesn't know what each person can do. Help him out.

PARTNER **A:** Ask which person can do the activity well.

PARTNER **B:** Answer according to the picture. (girl or boy)

—¿Quién baila muy bien, Diego o Carlota?
—*Él* baila muy bien.

¿Quién patina muy bien, Jorge o Elena?

1.

¿Quién pinta muy bien, Luis o Rita?

2.

3. ¿Quién camina mucho, Manuel o Amalia?

 4. ¿Quién estudia mucho, Susana o Gregorio?

 **5.** ¿Quién nada muy bien, Víctor o Diana?

 6. ¿Quién baila muy bien, Agustín o Laura?

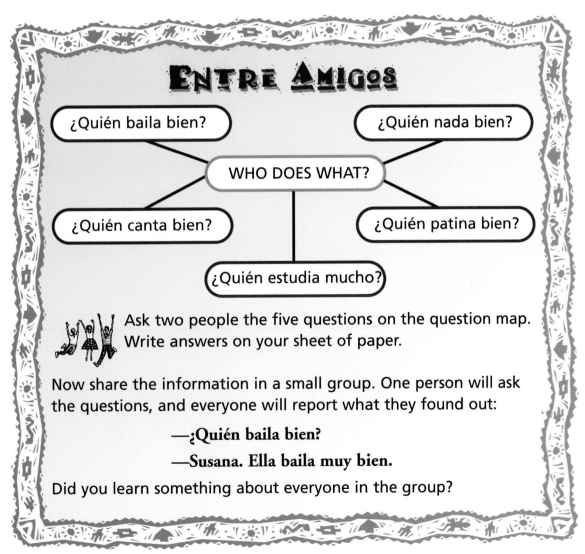

ENTRE AMIGOS

¿Quién baila bien?

¿Quién nada bien?

WHO DOES WHAT?

¿Quién canta bien?

¿Quién patina bien?

¿Quién estudia mucho?

Ask two people the five questions on the question map. Write answers on your sheet of paper.

Now share the information in a small group. One person will ask the questions, and everyone will report what they found out:

—**¿Quién baila bien?**

—**Susana. Ella baila muy bien.**

Did you learn something about everyone in the group?

¿Cómo lo dices?

Describing how often you do something

Do you always swim in June? Or sometimes walk to school in spring? Perhaps you never skate, not even in winter. Look at Daniel's schedules to see how to say things like this in Spanish.

L	M	M	J	V	S	D
●	●	●	●	●	●	●
●	●	●	●	●	●	●

L	M	M	J	V	S	D
●			●			
	●	●				●

L	M	M	J	V	S	D

Daniel **siempre** estudia
en la casa.

Daniel **a veces**
camina a la tienda.

Daniel **nunca** patina.

**Este artista vive en
Costa Rica.**

¿Nadas los fines de semana?

¡ÚSALO!

You're being interviewed by the school newspaper, and you patiently answer the reporter's questions about your activities.

PARTNER A: Ask the question.
PARTNER B: Say how often you do the activity.

—¿Usas la computadora en la escuela?
—**Sí, a veces uso la computadora.**

1. ¿Nadas los fines de semana en agosto?

2. ¿Cantas en la escuela?

3. ¿Patinas en el parque en el invierno?

4. ¿Practicas los deportes en mayo?

5. ¿Bailas los lunes?

6. ¿Pintas en el salón de clase?

7. ¿Caminas a la escuela?

8. ¿Estudias en la casa los domingos?

ENTRE AMIGOS

Birthdays and **santos** are just two of the days that people celebrate. Look at this list of different **días de fiesta:**

Año Nuevo	1 de enero
Día de los Novios	14 de febrero
Día de la Bandera (México)	24 de febrero
Día de San Patricio	17 de marzo
Día de la Madre	en el mes de mayo
Día de la Independencia	4 de julio
Aniversario del General San Martín (Argentina)	17 de agosto
Día de la Raza (Panamá)	12 de octubre
Día de los Veteranos	en el mes de noviembre
La Navidad	25 de diciembre

Get with a partner. Take turns picking different holidays. Say when the holiday is, and ask each other if you ever celebrate **(celebrar)** the holiday:

A: El día de San Patricio es el diecisiete de marzo. ¿Celebras tú el día de San Patricio?

B: Sí, a veces. ¿Y tú?

A: No, nunca celebro el día de San Patricio.

Guatemala. Hay un desfile para celebrar este día de fiesta.

San Antonio, Texas. Los niños celebran un cumpleaños.

¡A divertirnos!

 Make a piñata with a partner! Decide on a fun animal or creature to make, then follow these instructions:

1. Cut a newspaper into lots of strips 5 centimeters (2 inches) wide.

2. Blow up a balloon.

3. Dip the newspaper strips into a paste made from flour and water (one strip at a time). Cover the balloon with the newspaper strips. Make four layers of the strips in all.

4. Let the piñata dry until the paper is hard. Then decorate it with paint, colored paper, or other materials.

5. Cut a hole in the top of the piñata. Pop the balloon and remove it. Fill the inside of the piñata with wrapped candy, small toys, or anything else you think would be fun!

6. Now your piñata is ready to use! Hang it from the ceiling with a string. Take turns trying to break it open with a stick—and no peeking!

UNIDAD 7

•••• De mí y de ti

What do you talk about with your friends, classmates, and the grown-ups around you? You spend a lot of time telling them about yourself and finding out things about them, don't you?

You might talk about your age, for example, or say how you're feeling today. Or you might mention something special in your life, such as a birthday.

In this unit, you'll:

- Talk about how you are feeling and ask others about their feelings

- Tell your age and ask about the age of others

- Learn when to use **tú** and when to use **usted**

- Discuss some ways Spanish-speaking families celebrate birthdays

Una quinceañera en Venezuela

¡Qué hambre tengo!

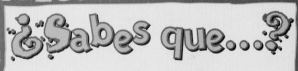

¿Sabes que...?

In Spanish-speaking countries:

● When a girl turns fifteen, her family treats her like a queen for a day. She's called a *quinceañera*. They may also throw a big party and invite all their friends and relatives.

● Politeness is a very highly valued quality. Often, young people are taught to stand when an adult enters the room and to remain standing until the person indicates they should sit.

¿De qué hablan ellos?

¡HABLEMOS!

What's the matter?

—¿Qué tienes?
—Tengo frío.

Tengo frío.

Tengo calor.

Tengo sed.

Tengo hambre.

—¿Y tú? ¿Qué tienes?

Tengo sueño.

Tengo dolor.

Tengo la gripe.

Tengo miedo.

Así es... Are you ever tired after a big lunch? A lot of people are! In a number of Spanish-speaking countries, many businesses close from about noon until 3:00 P.M. each day. This long break is called a *siesta*, and for many years people would use this time to take a nap before returning to work. Now most people use this break just to take a long lunch.

PRACTIQUEMOS

What a strange day! Every time you ask a friend about going to the park, he or she comes up with a different excuse.

PARTNER A: Ask your partner if he or she is going to the park today.

PARTNER B: Make an excuse according to the picture.

—¿Vas al parque hoy?
—No, no voy al parque. Tengo frío.

1.

2.

3.

4.

5.

6.

ENTRE AMIGOS

Form a group with three or four classmates. Use index cards and colored pencils or markers to make cue cards for your group. Invent your own pictures or symbols to show the eight different situations on pages 142–143.

Put the cards in a pile. Draw a card, but don't show it to the other players. The rest of your group must take turns asking questions to find out what is on your card.

—¿Tienes sueño?
—No, no tengo sueño.
  —¿Tienes miedo?
  —No, no tengo miedo.
—¿Tienes sed?
—Sí. Tengo sed.

When someone guesses correctly, show your card to the group, then return it to the bottom of the pile. The person who guessed correctly then gets to pick the next card, and the game continues. Play until your teacher tells you to stop.

¡HABLEMOS!

Is she in a hurry?

—¿Tiene ella prisa?

—Sí, tiene prisa.

Tiene prisa.

Tiene razón.

Tiene suerte.

—¿Cuántos años tiene?

—Tiene ochenta años.

—¿Verdad?

—Sí, hoy es su cumpleaños.

Tiene ochenta años.

¡Tienes diez años!

¿Cuántos años tiene la niña?

PRACTIQUEMOS

What do you notice about these people? Describe each picture using **tiene** and an appropriate word.

Raúl

Raúl tiene razón.

1.

Kyomi

2.

José

3.

Luisa

4.

Felipe

ENTRE AMIGOS

Bring pictures of members of your family from home. (Be sure your mom or dad says it's OK to bring the ones you choose.) The more people of different ages in the pictures, the better. If you like, you could also bring pictures from magazines and make up a "pretend" family.

With a partner, ask questions about the members of your families. Note down everything you learn about your partner's family. You and your partner should ask each other:

- each family member's name
- how old each family member is
- what the family member likes to do

Then use your partner's pictures and your notes to show and tell the class what you have learned.

—¿Cómo se llama?
—Se llama Peter Daniels.
    —¿Cuántos años tiene?
    —Tiene treinta y seis años.
—¿Qué le gusta hacer?
—Le gusta usar la computadora.

Una familia
colombiana

¿Cómo lo dices?

Talking with classmates and adults

In English, when we talk to someone, we use only one word—"you." In Spanish there are two ways to say "you." Look carefully at the people in the pictures and read the sentences. Which word is used for "you"?

Tú bailas muy bien.

Tú nadas muy bien.

Tú cantas muy bien.

Now study these pictures and sentences. Which word is used for "you"?

Señor, ¿cómo se llama **usted?**

Señora, **usted** camina mucho.

Can you see the difference between **tú** and **usted?** Use **tú** with people who are your own age or younger, as well as with friends and family members. Use **usted** with older persons and people you don't know.

Did you also notice that the verb forms change, too? These verbs end in **-as** with **tú** and in **-a** with **usted.**

¡ÚSALO!

A. Aren't the people around you amazing? Everyone seems to be full of surprises and talents. Tell each person that he or she does the activity very well. Use **tú** or **usted**.

¡Señor Martínez! ¡Usted patina muy bien!

Señor Martínez

1. Margarita

2. Pablo

3. Señor López

4. Señora Parra

5. Señorita Vargas

6. David

B. A group of students and teachers from South America is visiting your school, and you want to ask them some questions. Decide which question you'd use for each of these people.

> Señor Escobar
> a. ¿Cómo te llamas tú?
> b. ¿Cómo se llama usted?   **b. ¿Cómo se llama usted?**

1. Alejandro Peña
   a. ¿Cómo está usted?
   b. ¿Cómo estás tú?

2. Señorita Cortez
   a. ¿Usa la computadora?
   b. ¿Usas la computadora?

3. María Elena Solís
   a. ¿Vas tú a la clase de música?
   b. ¿Va usted a la clase de música?

4. Luis Baroja
   a. ¿Practica los deportes?
   b. ¿Practicas los deportes?

5. Señora Vásquez
   a. ¿Qué haces tú en agosto?
   b. ¿Qué hace usted en agosto?

6. Javier Castillo
   a. ¿Va al cine los sábados?
   b. ¿Vas al cine los sábados?

¿Qué usas, tú o usted?

C. Imagine that you are a visiting teacher from Central America. Your partner is a student at your school. You are having a conversation. Read the parts and complete the conversations with **tú** or **usted.** Then switch roles.

ALUMNA: ¿Cómo se llama **usted?**

PROFESOR: Me llamo el señor Goya. ¿Cómo te llamas _____?

ALUMNA: Me llamo Gloria Castillo. ¿Le gusta la escuela?

PROFESOR: Sí, me gusta mucho. ¿_____ estudias mucho?

ALUMNA: No, no me gusta estudiar mucho. Me gusta el verano. ¿Qué hace _____ en el verano?

PROFESOR: Siempre nado y camino en el verano. ¿Qué haces _____ en el verano?

ALUMNA: También me gusta nadar. ¿Va _____ al cine a veces?

PROFESOR: Sí, voy al cine todos los sábados. Nunca voy los domingos. ¿Vas _____ al cine?

ALUMNA: Sí, siempre me gusta ir al cine.

Hugo es el amigo de Ramón.

ENTRE AMIGOS

Think of the names of two different people. They should be people known to everyone in the class. Try to include people of different ages. Write each name on a separate piece of paper. Use complete names and titles such as **Doctor** or **Señor,** if appropriate.

Place all the names in a bag. Pass the bag around the class and take turns drawing one at a time. Read the name aloud and make up one sentence or question that you would use if you met that person.

Señorita Mariah Carey
¿Usted usa la computadora mucho?

¿CÓMO LO DICES?

Saying what you have and how you are

Sometimes you use the verb **tener** to talk about "having something." Look at these sentences.

Tengo dos libros.

¿**Tienes** tú un globo?

Sara **tiene** un lápiz.

You can also use **tener** to talk about how you are or how you feel.

Tengo calor.

¿Tienes calor?

¿Tiene usted calor?

Él **tiene** calor.

Ella **tiene** calor.

Did you notice how **tener** changes depending on which person it is used with? If you use it to talk about yourself, the form is **tengo.** When you're talking to a friend, it's **tienes,** and with an adult, it's **tiene.** Also, when you're talking about another person, it's **tiene.**

These different forms are used even if you don't actually say or write the words **yo, tú, usted, él,** or **ella.**

Festival del Cinco de Mayo, San Francisco, California

¡ÚSALO!

A. You and some of your friends put on a pet fair at Luis Pike's house. Now, Mrs. Pike is trying to figure out who has the pets so they get home okay. Help her.

PARTNER A: Ask if your partner has the pet(s).
PARTNER B: Answer according to the indicated clue.

—¿Tienes tú los loros verdes?
(Ricardo)
—No, Señora. Ricardo tiene los loros verdes.

1. ¿Tienes tú la mariposa verde? (Claudia)

2. ¿Tienes tú el gato gris? (Usted)

3. ¿Tienes tú los tres canarios? (Leonardo)

4. ¿Tienes tú el perro negro? (Nicolás)

5. ¿Tienes tú el loro azul? (Yo)

6. ¿Tienes tú los cuatro peces? (Ernestina)

Los alumnos son de Caracas, Venezuela. ¿Tiene hambre o tiene sed el muchacho? ¿Qué tiene la muchacha?

B. You're very concerned because everyone at school seems to be having a problem. Find out what's wrong.

PARTNER A:	Complete the question and ask what's wrong.
PARTNER B:	Answer according to the picture.

—Adela, ¿qué tienes?
—Tengo mucho frío.

Adela, ¿qué_____?

1. Señor Otero, ¿qué _____ usted?

2. Eva, ¿qué _____ el señor Ibarra?

3. Inés, ¿qué _____ Pablo?

4. Mario, ¿qué _____ Rosa?

5. César, ¿qué _____?

6. Julia, ¿qué _____ tú?

¿Te gusta la televisión?
¿Cuál es tu programa favorito?

C. It's your big day! You're a contestant on a TV game show. For every answer they give you, you must give a corresponding question.

La señora Prado tiene sesenta y tres años.
¿Cuántos años tiene la señora Prado?

1. Sí, Humberto tiene frío.

2. No, Amalia no tiene hambre.

3. Sí, tengo mucha sed.

4. Tengo cincuenta años.

5. No, Sandra no tiene sueño.

6. Sí, tienes mucha prisa.

7. Tengo nueve años.

8. Sí, Mercedes tiene razón.

9. No, Rogelio no tiene la gripe.

10. No, el señor Ortiz no tiene suerte.

D. Why not find out how a classmate is doing today? Choose a partner and make up three questions to ask him or her using **tener.** Then answer your partner's questions.

—¿Tienes frío hoy?
—No, no tengo frío hoy.
   —¿Tienes mucha suerte hoy?
   —Sí, tengo suerte.
—¿Tienes dolor hoy?
—No, hoy no tengo dolor.

¿Tienes hambre?

ENTRE AMIGOS

Practice using **tener** quickly! The whole class will stand in a circle. Your teacher will give you something to hold: an object or objects, a picture of an object, or a card.

If you get an object or a picture, hold it so the rest of the class can see it. If you get a card, it will have an expression on it like **tengo miedo** or **tengo sed.** In that case, act out the expression so the rest of the class knows what card you have.

Your teacher will direct you either to say something about what you're holding or to ask a question. Whenever someone asks a **quién** question, the whole class must answer it.

TEACHER: Julia - Yo
JULIA: Yo tengo dos libros.

TEACHER: Marcos - Yo
MARCOS: Yo tengo miedo.

TEACHER: Sara - quién - miedo
SARA: ¿Quién tiene miedo?
CLASS: Marcos tiene miedo.

TEACHER: Samuel - Luis - qué
SAMUEL: Luis, ¿qué tienes?
LUIS: Tengo un lápiz.

TEACHER: Ana - quién - dos libros
ANA: ¿Quién tiene dos libros?
CLASS: Julia tiene dos libros.

The idea is to skip around the circle and go fast! If you make a mistake, the person to your left has to say the sentence correctly. Now, hurry up, and good luck!

¡A divertirnos!

Do you know someone who's having a birthday soon? Maybe you just have a good friend to whom you'd like to send a nice wish. Everyone likes that!

Use your artistic talents and some of the Spanish you've learned in this unit to make a greeting card. It doesn't matter if your friend speaks Spanish or not, because you do, and you can explain your card! Here are some other phrases you might use:

Get well soon!
¡Que te mejores pronto!

Happy Birthday!
¡Feliz cumpleaños!

Congratulations!
¡Felicitaciones!

Best wishes!
¡Deseándote lo mejor!

¿Qué hora es?

Have you ever wondered what it would be like to go through a day in school without clocks, watches, or schedules?

And think what would happen if there were no clocks to tell time when you got home. When you stop to think about it, our world would be turned upside down if there were no way to tell time.

In this unit, you'll learn to:

- Ask and tell what time it is
- Say at what time you do different things
- Talk about how long activities last
- Talk about schedules
- Ask different types of questions

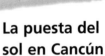

La puesta del
sol en Cancún

Un horario de vuelos en
la Ciudad de México

¿Es grande o es
pequeño este reloj?

¡HABLEMOS!

How much time is there?

—¿Cuánto tiempo hay en un cuarto de hora?
—Hay quince minutos en un cuarto de hora.

un minuto

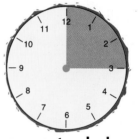

un cuarto de hora

una media hora

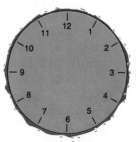

una hora

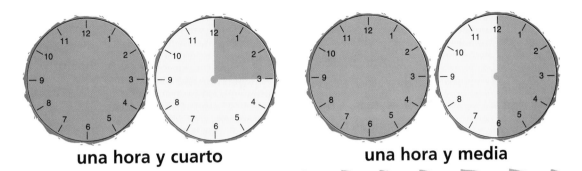

una hora y cuarto　　　**una hora y media**

—¿Cuántas horas hay en un día?

—Hay veinticuatro horas en un día.

Así es... The meaning of "on time" varies from culture to culture. In some cultures, punctuality is very important. In others, people are more relaxed about punctuality. For example, in Spain people tend to arrive for events at the precise time. In Mexico, "on time" *(a tiempo)* can mean within fifteen minutes or so of the time. In Peru, if you are *a tiempo* for a party starting at 8:00, you might not arrive until 10:00. People often refer to this idea of time as the *hora latina*.

PRACTIQUEMOS

Susana made a chart showing what she's going to do each day after school. Her chart has clocks that help her see how much time she'll spend doing each thing. Read Susana's chart, then answer the questions.

ACTIVIDAD	TIEMPO
Voy a practicar deportes.	
Voy a cantar.	
Voy a caminar.	
Voy a estudiar.	
Voy a nadar.	
Voy a usar la computadora.	

¿Cuánto tiempo va a nadar Susana?
Va a nadar una hora.

1. ¿Cuánto tiempo va a practicar deportes Susana?

2. ¿Cuánto tiempo va a estudiar Susana?

3. ¿Cuánto tiempo va a caminar Susana?

4. ¿Cuánto tiempo va a cantar Susana?

5. ¿Cuánto tiempo va a usar la computadora Susana?

ENTRE AMIGOS

Make your own chart like Susana's. Choose five things you're going to do today or tomorrow and write a sentence for each one, like this: **Voy a patinar.** Your teacher will help you if you don't know a word for an activity.

Next to each sentence, draw a clock or clocks to show how long you plan to do that activity:

Voy a patinar.

Now, get together with a partner and ask each other questions about your charts:

—¿Qué vas a hacer mañana?
—Voy a patinar.
—¿Cuánto tiempo vas a patinar?
—Voy a patinar media hora.

¿Vas a nadar mañana?

What time of the day is it?

—¿Cuándo vas a la biblioteca?

—Voy por la tarde.

la noche

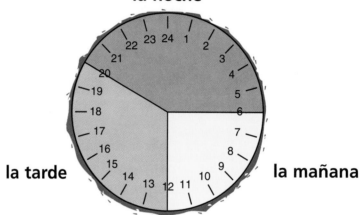

la tarde

la mañana

el mediodía

la medianoche

—¿Caminas en el parque a la medianoche?

—No, no camino a la medianoche.

la salida del sol

la puesta del sol

**¿Cómo es el reloj,
viejo o moderno?**

Así es...

Although there is no precise rule, when Spanish-speakers talk about *la tarde*, they can mean any time from noon to about 8:00 P.M. There aren't separate words for "afternoon" and "evening."

Practiquemos

Which time of day goes best with the sentences below? Look at the pictures and decide. You can use a time more than once.

 **A.**  **B.**  **C.**  **D.**

Tengo frío. No hace sol. No es la tarde.
d. la medianoche

1. ¡Tengo prisa! Camino a la escuela.

2. No es la mañana. Tengo hambre. Hace mucho sol.

3. ¡Buenas noches! Tengo mucho sueño. No hace sol.

4. Voy a casa. Voy a estudiar. No hay mucho sol.

5. ¡Buenos días! El pájaro canta.

La salida del sol es muy tranquila.

ENTRE AMIGOS

Write down three different things you do:

Bailo, Voy a la escuela, Nado, Voy al cine, etc.

Now, put down the time of day that you do these three things:

Bailo – por la noche
Voy a la escuela – por la mañana

Form a circle with three or four classmates. One person starts by saying something he or she does **(Bailo)**. The rest of the group tries to guess when **(por la mañana, por la tarde, por la noche)** by asking a question. They decide on the time they think is correct and ask:

¿Bailas por la tarde?

The first person responds according to what he or she wrote.

No, no bailo por la tarde. Bailo por la noche.

In this case, the first person gets a point because the others guessed wrong. If the others guessed correctly, they would receive the point. Keep taking turns and play to five points.

¿Vas a la escuela por la mañana?

Sí, voy a la escuela por la mañana.

¿CÓMO LO DICES?

What time is it?

Look at these sentences to see how you can answer the
question **¿Qué hora es?**

¡Es la una!

¡Son las dos!

¡Es la una y veinte!

¡Son las siete y cuarto!

¡Son las seis y media!

¡Son las once y veinticinco!

You use **es** with **la una** and times that include **la una,** and
you use **son** with all the other times or hours.

But how do you stress that it's a certain time exactly, or link the time to a part of the day? Look at these sentences.

¡Es la una **en punto**!

Son las siete **de la mañana**.

Son las tres y cuarto **de la tarde**.

Son las nueve **de la noche**.

¿A qué hora es la puesta del sol—a las nueve de la noche o a las nueve de la mañana?

A. Today is going very slowly for Samuel. He asks you the time at least a million times! But you're patient, so each time he asks **¿Qué hora es?** you look at your watch and answer.

Son las ocho y media.

1.

2.

3.

4.

5.

6.

7.

8.

9.

B. Your watch sometimes runs fast, sometimes slow. Fortunately, your friend has an accurate watch to give you the time.

| PARTNER **A:** | Ask if the time on your watch is correct. |
| PARTNER **B:** | You're the friend. Answer according to your watch. |

 —¿Son las diez y cuarto?
—No. Son las diez y dieciséis.

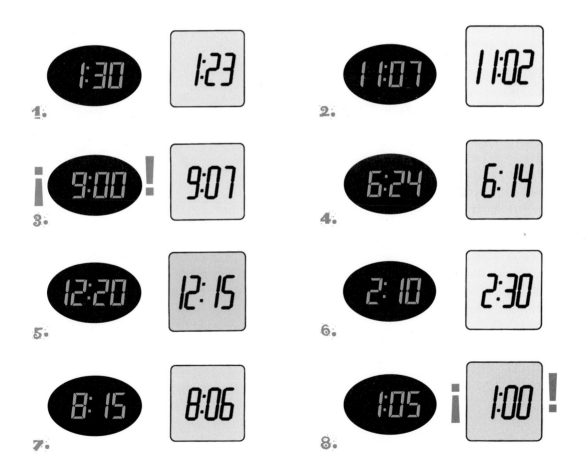

1.

2.

3.

4.

5.

6.

7.

8.

¿CÓMO LO DICES?

Telling time another way

You've already been telling time in Spanish. Now look at these times and notice what is different.

¡Es la una **menos** cuarto!

¡Son las cuatro **menos** diez!

¡Son las siete **menos** veintitrés!

¡Son las doce **menos** veinte!

When you use **menos** you are subtracting the number of minutes between the number 12 and the minute hand. It's similar to what we say in English: "It's twenty to twelve." Use **menos** when the time is between the half hour and the next hour on the clock.

To ask and answer questions about when people are going to do different things, you can use **¿A qué hora...?** or **¿Cuándo...?**

—¿**A qué hora** caminas a la escuela?
—A las ocho menos veinte de la mañana.

—¿**A qué hora** va a bailar Diana?
—Diana va a bailar a las cinco menos cuarto.

—¿**Cuándo** vas a cantar?
—Voy a cantar a las nueve menos diez de la noche.

When you answer questions about the time when someone is going to do something, be sure to use the word **a** before the time.

A. Your friend forgot her glasses and she can't see the clock. Answer her question ¿**Qué hora es?** for each of the times.

Es la una menos cuarto.

 1.

 2.

 3.

 4.

5.

6.

 7.

 8.

B. It's Friday afternoon and you're talking with a friend about the different things you'll be doing on Saturday.

PARTNER A: Ask when your friend will be doing the indicated activity.

PARTNER B: Answer according to the time.

ir al parque / 4:40   —¿A qué hora vas al parque?
—**Voy al parque a las cinco menos veinte.**

1. nadar / 1:45   **5.** ir a casa / 5:55
2. estudiar / 7:37   **6.** pintar / 2:50
3. ir al cine / 12:35   **7.** practicar los deportes / 9:46
4. usar la computadora / 11:31   **8.** cantar / 10:40

C. You're trying to get together with your friends, so you need to know their schedules.

PARTNER A: Ask the question.

PARTNER B: Answer according to the times in parentheses.

—¿Cuándo vas a la biblioteca?
(2:15 P.M.)
—**A las dos y cuarto de la tarde.**

1. ¿Cuándo vas al cine?
(8:30 P.M.)

2. ¿Cuándo vas al gimnasio?
(9:15 P.M.)

3. ¿Cuándo vas a bailar?
(11:35 A.M.)

4. ¿Cuándo vas a nadar?
(3:55 P.M.)

5. ¿Cuándo vas a estudiar?
(2:30 P.M.)

6. ¿Cuándo vas a patinar?
(10:40 A.M.)

D. Verónica and Víctor are very busy twins. Their mother has to tape their Saturday schedules on the refrigerator!

PARTNER A: Ask the questions about the twins' schedules.

PARTNER B: Answer according to the schedule.

—¿A qué hora va él al cine?
—Él va al cine a las siete y cinco de la tarde.

Verónica		Víctor	
8:30 a.m.	la clase de música	9:00 a.m.	el gimnasio
10:45 a.m.	la biblioteca	11:35 a.m.	la clase de computadoras
1:50 p.m.	el cine	1:15 p.m.	la clase de arte
8:45 p.m.	la casa de la Sra. Millán	7:05 p.m.	el cine

1. ¿A qué hora va ella a la clase de música?
2. ¿A qué hora va él a la clase de computadoras?
3. ¿Cuándo va ella a la biblioteca?
4. ¿Cuándo va él a la clase de arte?
5. ¿Cuándo va ella a la casa de la señora Millán?
6. ¿Cuándo va ella al cine?
7. ¿A qué hora va él al gimnasio?

ENTRE AMIGOS

First, divide the class into two teams. Each team will make its own clock. You'll need a paper plate, a metal fastener, construction paper, and a crayon or marker.

Write the numbers 1–12 around the inside of the plate, so it looks like a clock. Cut a long and a short hand for the clock from construction paper and fasten them to the center of the plate.

Now play the "Time Game." Turn your desks around so the teams are facing each other.

Take turns. Put a time on your clock and ask someone on the other team what time they are going to do something:

¿A qué hora vas a bailar?

The person on the other team must answer with the time on your clock:

Voy a bailar a las cinco menos diez.

If the answer is correct, the other team scores one point. If the answer is wrong, the person next to you gets one chance to correct it, and then your team scores the point.

The first team to score ten points wins!

¿Cómo lo dices?

Asking for information

Some questions only ask for yes-no answers:

¿Vas al cine? ¿Estudias mucho? ¿Tienes suerte?

Other types of questions ask for more information, such as a time of day, a color, or a place. To ask these kinds of questions, you need question words. Different question words ask for different information. You've already been practicing these kinds of questions throughout this book:

¿Qué es esto?

¿Cómo te llamas?

¿Quién es el muchacho?

¿Cuándo vas a estudiar?

¿Cuál es tu número de teléfono?

¿A qué hora va a nadar Jorge?

¿Cuántos bolígrafos tienes tú?

¿De qué color es tu perro?

¿Cuánto tiempo vas a usar
la computadora?

¿Adónde vas?

¿Qué hora es?

Notice that the question words come at the beginning of the question. Where does the word indicating the person or thing being referred to—**Jorge, tú, perro**—come in the question?

¡ÚSALO!

A. You're playing a game of "What's the Question?" with your friends. The object of the game is to choose the question that goes with the answer.

El ratón es pequeño.
a.   ¿Cómo se llama el ratón?
b.   ¿De qué color es el ratón?
c.   ¿Cómo es el ratón?   **c. ¿Cómo es el ratón?**

1. Voy a la escuela.
  a. ¿Cuándo vas tú?
  b. ¿Adónde vas?
  c. ¿A qué hora vas?

2. Me llamo Esteban Llosa.
  a. ¿Quién es el muchacho?
  b. ¿Qué es esto?
  c. ¿Cómo te llamas?

3. Son las tres menos cuarto.
  a. ¿Qué día es hoy?
  b. ¿A qué hora estudias?
  c. ¿Qué hora es?

4. Tengo veinte loros.
  a. ¿Cuántos loros tienes?
  b. ¿Qué son estos?
  c. ¿Cómo son los loros?

5. Estudio a las diez.
  a. ¿Qué hora es?
  b. ¿Adónde vas?
  c. ¿A qué hora va a estudiar usted?

6. Es el salón de clase.
  a. ¿Cuándo vas a la clase?
  b. ¿Qué es esto?
  c. ¿Quién es?

¿Qué es el tiempo?
El tiempo es oro.

B. You and a friend are with a visitor from Venezuela. The visitor keeps asking you questions, but the school band is practicing next door, and you can only hear part of the questions. Your friend has to repeat the whole question.

PARTNER A: Complete and ask the entire question.
PARTNER B: Answer the question truthfully.

> ¿_____ hora vas a la escuela?
>
> —¿**A qué hora vas a la escuela?**
> —**Voy a la escuela a las ocho y media.**

1. ¿_____ te llamas?

2. ¿_____ años tienes?

3. ¿_____ es tu profesor?

4. ¿_____ hora estudias en casa?

5. ¿_____ alumnos hay en tu clase de arte?

6. ¿_____ estación te gusta?

7. ¿_____ tiempo hace en el verano?

8. ¿_____ vas esta semana?

9. ¿_____ color es tu perro?

10. ¿_____ vas al parque?

Una banda escolar en España. ¿Te gusta la música?

ENTRE AMIGOS

Almost everywhere you go, watching television is a popular pastime. In Spanish-speaking countries, in addition to the shows made in Spanish, you can often see programs (**los programas**) that were made in the U.S. The only difference is that they've been dubbed in Spanish.

Look at the sample television guide below with a partner. How many programs can you recognize?

Use the question words you've learned and write at least five questions about the guide. Use as many different kinds of questions as you can. Join another pair of students and take turns asking them your questions. Then answer theirs.

Telehorario: Sábado, 19 de febrero

8:00 El coche fantástico
Las aventuras de Miguel y su coche negro, KITT.

9:00 Documental: Dinosaurios
Antonio Sarapo habla de los dinosaurios.

9:30 Sábado mañana
Variedades. La orquesta Sol y Sombra canta "El verano en México" y Pepe López canta y baila "La bamba".

10:00 La pantera rosa
La pantera rosa va a la escuela.

10:30 La conquista del espacio
El capitán Kirk va al planeta Vulcano con el señor Spock.

11:30 Profesor Poopsnagle
"El misterio de la casa negra." El profesor va con Matt a Puerto Rico para investigar la misteriosa casa negra.

12:00 Especial de deportes
El béisbol en la República Dominicana.

¡A divertirnos!

How good are your powers of concentration? Your teacher has taped thirty-six numbered cards to the board. There are questions on the backs of eighteen of them. The answers to the questions are on the other eighteen cards. Your challenge is to match questions with answers.

Form two teams with your classmates. A student from Team A calls out a number. The teacher shows that card to everyone, and then the student reads it aloud.

The same student calls out a second number. The teacher shows that card and the student reads it aloud. Is it a match? If it is, Team A scores a point. The same student keeps playing until he or she fails to make a match.

If the two cards don't match, the teacher will put them back where they were, and it's Team B's turn.

Continue until all the questions are matched with their answers. The team with the most matches wins.

Mis clases favoritas...

You and your friends probably talk about school a lot. It's only natural, since you spend a lot of time there. And that doesn't include homework!

Well, Spanish-speaking kids talk about school a lot, too!

In this unit, you'll:

- Talk about classes you like *(and* classes you don't like!)
- Give your opinion about different things
- Talk about your likes and dislikes
- Talk about things you do in school

¡Es la hora del recreo!

Un alumno
colombiano

Alumnos en España

¿Sabes que...?

In Spanish-speaking countries:

- The most popular foreign language course is English.

- Many activities like sports, art, and music often aren't sponsored by schools. Kids do them at local clubs.

- Classes usually begin between 7 A.M. and 8 A.M. and last until 3 P.M. or 4 P.M.

- Kids in fourth grade study about 9 or 10 different subjects each week!

¡HABLEMOS!

What's your favorite class?

—¿Cuál es tu clase favorita?

—¡El español, claro!

el español

LIBRO

las ciencias

la salud

BOOK

el inglés

$$\begin{array}{r} 20.5 \\ \times\ 4.6 \\ \hline 94.3 \end{array}$$

las matemáticas

la geografía

la educación física

las ciencias
sociales

Esta escuela está en
Hidalgo, México.

PRACTIQUEMOS

Your teacher has just put up a bulletin board with photos of students in their favorite classes. Find out which subjects your friends like.

PARTNER A: Ask what each student's favorite class is.
PARTNER B: Answer according to the pictures.

Chela

—¿Cuál es la clase favorita de Chela?
—¡Es la geografía, claro!

1. Fernando

2. Jaime

3. Lucía

4. Óscar

5. Toña

6. Elisa

ENTRE AMIGOS

 Now ask three people in your class this question:

Y tú, ¿cuál es tu clase favorita?

Keep track of your answers.

Now work with the rest of your class. Pick one of your classmates to go to the blackboard and make a chart that looks like this:

One student calls out the name of a person in the class. If you hear the name of someone you interviewed, say what that person's favorite class is. The person at the blackboard adds the information to the chart.

When everybody's name has been called, add up the answers. What are the five most popular classes?

¡HABLEMOS!

What's your opinion?

¡La clase es fantástica!

—¿Te gusta la clase de ciencias?

—Sí, me gusta mucho.

—¿Por qué?

—¡Es fantástica!

¡La clase es aburrida!

—¿Te gusta la clase de salud?

—¡Ay, no!

—¿Por qué no?

—¡Es aburrida!

¡Es fácil!

¡Es difícil!

—¿Qué piensas tú?

—¡Es importante!

¡Es importante!

¡Es interesante!

¡Es terrible!

¡Es divertido!

Alumnas venezolanas

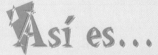

Así es...

When Spanish-speaking students really like something, they may also say:

¡Es sensacional!

¡Es fabuloso!

¡Es maravilloso!

¡Es espectacular!

PRACTIQUEMOS

You're a very good observer. Look at these people. What will they answer if you ask them **¿Cómo es?**

Es divertido.

1.

2.

3.

4.

5.

6.

ENTRE AMIGOS

 Draw pictures of yourself in two different classes—a class you like a lot and a class you don't like as much. The drawings should show:

- **what class you're in**
- **how you feel about that class**

Don't write any words on your drawings.

Then get together with a partner and trade drawings. Try to guess which class is shown in each drawing. Then try to guess how your partner feels about that class.

Here's an example:

A: ¿Es la clase de ciencias?
B: No…
A: ¿Es la clase de salud?
B: Sí, es la clase de salud.

A: ¿Y la clase de salud es interesante?
B: No…
A: ¿Por qué? ¿Es aburrida?
B: ¡Sí, es muy aburrida!

¿CÓMO LO DICES?

Talking about things you like

You already know how to talk about something you like:

Me gusta el libro.

A Inés **le gusta** el loro.

¿Te gusta el pez?

But what happens when there's more than one thing?
Look at these examples:

Me gustan los libros.

A Inés **le gustan** los loros.

¿Te gustan los peces?

Did you notice that you say **gustan** instead of **gusta**
when you're talking about more than one thing?

**¿Te gustan los colores
de este carrito?**

¡ÚSALO!

A. Mario is always in a good mood. He likes everything you talk to him about. Complete his statements. (Sometimes you'll need **gusta** and sometimes you'll need **gustan.**)

¡Me _____ los libros!
¡Me gustan los libros!

1. ¡Me _____ la historia!

2. ¡Me _____ las matemáticas!

3. ¡Me _____ las clases!

4. ¡Me _____ la muchacha!

B. Mario's friend Marcos is in a bad mood today. He doesn't like *anything* you talk to him about!

¡ ___ me _____ los libros!
¡No me gustan los libros!

1. ¡ ____me _____ las mariposas!

2. ¡ ___ me _____ el arte!

3. ¡ ___ me _____ la biblioteca!

4. ¡ ___ me _____ los animales!

ESPAÑOL Y LITERATURA	A	B	I	B	A
Lectura	A	B+	B	B	
Vocabulario	B	E	I	B+	
Gramática	B	A	I	B	
Ortografía	I	A	I	I	
Composición	I	E	A	B+	
INGLES	B+	B	I	B+	B
Lectura	B+	B	B	B+	
Ortografía	A	I	I	B	
Composición	B+	B+	B+	B+	
Lenguaje	B	B+	I	B+	
Fonética	B+	B+	I	B	
Escritura	E	B+	B+	E	
MATEMATICAS	B+	B	B	A	B
Conceptos	E	A	B	A	
Cálculo Mental	E	B	A	B+	
Solución de Problemas	B+	B+	B	I	
Velocidad	B+	B+	B	B	
Habilidad de Transferencia	B	B	B	I	
Precisión	B	A	E	B+	
Esfuerzo	B+	B	A	B	

Un boletín de evaluación de una escuela colombiana

ENTRE AMIGOS

Here's your chance to find out what your friends like and don't like.

Take a piece of paper. You need to make a list of six items to ask about. Look at the the six categories shown below. Choose an item that fits each one. Write the items on your paper.

Ask a partner if he or she likes the things on your list:

—¿Te gusta (el español)?
—¡Sí, me gusta mucho! OR No, no me gusta.

Write down the answers. When the teacher calls your partner's name, tell everyone in the class what you've learned about your partner.

A Tomás no le gusta (el español). Le gusta mucho (la educación física).

Categories:
1. A school subject you think everyone likes

2. A school subject you think no one likes

3. An animal you think everyone likes

4. An animal that some people like and others don't

5. A day of the week

6. A season of the year

¿CÓMO LO DICES?

What do you do in school?

What's the main reason you come to school? To learn things! The verb that means "to learn" is **aprender**. Here's how you use it:

Aprendo el español.

¿**Aprendes** el español?

¿**Aprende** usted el español?

Él **aprende** el español.

Ella **aprende** el español.

Did you notice the different endings on the verb?

The verb **escribir** means "to write." Here's how you use it:

Escribo en la pizarra.

Tú **escribes** en la pizarra también.

Usted **escribe** en la pizarra.

Él **escribe** en la pizarra.

Ella **escribe** en la pizarra.

Most verbs that end in **-er** and **-ir** use these same endings, so if you know the endings for one verb, you know the endings for all the verbs in that group.

For example, the verb **leer** means "to read." How would you tell someone that you're reading a book? How would you ask a friend if she's reading?

Another important verb to know when you're learning Spanish is **comprender**, which means "to understand."

—**¿Comprendes?**
—**No, no comprendo.** OR **¡Sí, comprendo!**

A. Your little cousin Evita is pestering you with a lot of
questions. Try to be patient as you answer her. Answer yes
or no according to the picture.

—¿Aprendes el español?
—**Sí, aprendo el español.**

1. ¿Aprendes las matemáticas?

2. ¿Aprendes las ciencias sociales?

3. ¿Lees mucho en la clase de inglés?

4. ¿Comprendes la geografía?

5. ¿Escribes en el cuaderno?

6. ¿Lees libros en el gimnasio?

7. ¿Escribes en la pizarra?

8. ¿Comprendes las ciencias?

Un abuelo

B. Grandparents love to ask you questions about what you're learning at school, don't they? But sometimes they ask strange questions! With a partner, play the role of a grandparent, and ask what your "grandchild" is learning.

PARTNER A: Ask if your grandchild is learning each thing listed.

PARTNER B: You're the grandchild. Answer yes or no.

| a bailar | —**Miguelito, ¿aprendes a bailar en la escuela?**
—**No, no aprendo a bailar en la escuela.** |

1. las matemáticas
2. a cantar
3. a pintar
4. las ciencias
5. a patinar
6. a usar las computadoras
7. las ciencias sociales
8. la geografía
9. el español
10. a nadar

C. Now your grandparent wants to know the same things about your brother! Switch roles and ask the questions this way:

—Y Marcos, ¿aprende a bailar en la escuela?
—No, no aprende a bailar.

D. What is everyone reading in the library today? Ask your partner.

PARTNER A: Ask what each person is reading.
PARTNER B: Say what book the person is reading.

el Sr. Gómez / deportes   —¿Qué lee el Sr. Gómez?
                            —Lee un libro de deportes.

1. Javier / arte
2. Carolina / computadoras
3. la Sra. Martín / música

4. tú / geografía
5. Marta / español
6. Alejandro / ciencias sociales

¿Qué hace el estudiante?

¡Me gusta nadar!

 E. A television crew has come into your school. You are showing them around. They ask you what people are doing. Tell them.

la alumna / aprender la lección de ciencias sociales
—**¿Qué hace la alumna?**
—**Aprende la lección de ciencias sociales.**

1. la muchacha / escribir en un cuaderno
2. el profesor / escribir en un papel
3. el alumno / aprender las ciencias
4. la Srta. Blanco / leer
5. la muchacha / aprender el inglés
6. el muchacho / leer un libro de español

ENTRE AMIGOS

Your class is having an essay contest. The subject is "My Favorite Class." Here's Amalia's essay:

It's your turn! Write an essay about your favorite class. It should be about as long as Amalia's. To make yours even better, why not draw a picture to go with it?

Now get in a group of five classmates. Each person reads his or her essay, then the group decides which one it likes best. Finally, compare your group's favorite with that of other groups.

Mi clase favorita

Me gusta mucho la clase de matemáticas. No es difícil. Aprendo mucho en la clase. Leo el libro y comprendo la lección. Escribo los números en el cuaderno.

¡Es fantástico!
¡Siempre tengo razón!

Alumnos uruguayos

¡A divertirnos!

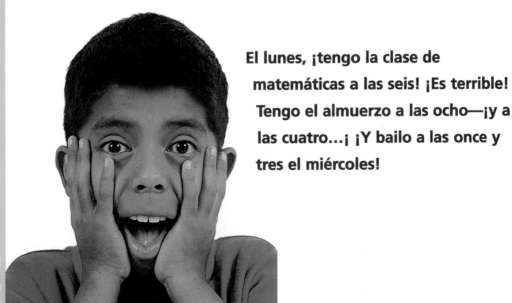

The new principal in your school has decided that the students will make up the schedules for next year's classes!

Draw the name of one of your classmates out of a paper bag. You have to create a schedule for that classmate. (You can be as creative as you want.)

Now draw up a chart with the days of the week across the top and the times for classes down the side. Then fill in a week's schedule. Maybe there will be classes on Saturdays! Maybe some classes will start very early in the morning and others will start very late at night. Some classes may last for hours, while others may last only for minutes! Maybe there will be some "unusual" classes…and don't forget lunch (**el almuerzo**) and recess (**el recreo**)!

When you're done, hand the schedule to your classmate. Take turns reading your schedules to one another.

El lunes, ¡tengo la clase de matemáticas a las seis! ¡Es terrible! Tengo el almuerzo a las ocho—¡y a las cuatro…¡ ¡Y bailo a las once y tres el miércoles!

Mi familia y yo

When you hear the word "family," what do you think of?

Some people think of parents and children. Others think of all the relatives, including cousins and grandparents. However you think of it, a family is important—it's people who care about each other.

In this unit, you'll:

- Learn the words for the members of a family
- Talk about who owns things
- Learn to use special names that show you care about people or things
- Learn about families in Spanish-speaking countries

¡Qué boda tan linda!

Una madre con su hijo

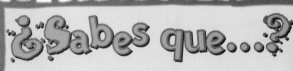

¿Sabes que...?

In Spanish-speaking countries:

- People often spend Sunday afternoons with aunts, uncles, cousins, and grandparents.

- People tend to name their children after other family members.

- Brothers, sisters, and cousins frequently socialize together, going to parties, the movies, shopping, and other places.

Mi abuelito

¡HABLEMOS!

What are their names?

—¿Cómo se llama la mamá de Alicia?

—Su mamá se llama Beatriz Muñoz.

Javier Muñoz Beatriz Muñoz

Mi papá Mi mamá

Mis papás

Los Muñoz

Alicia
Yo

Felipe
Mi hermano

Adriana
Mi hermana

Rosa
Mi hermanita

Mis hermanos y yo

Here are some additional words that describe other family members:

el padrastro – stepfather   **el hermanastro** – stepbrother
la madrastra – stepmother   **la hermanastra** – stepsister

Así es... A child in a Spanish-speaking country uses the last name of each parent. For example, if Jorge García Luna and his wife, Ana María Méndez de García, have a little girl named María Luz, her full name is María Luz García Méndez. The father's family name always comes first.

PRACTIQUEMOS

A. Look at Linda's family tree. Answer the questions.

Juan Gajardo   **Susana Gajardo**

  Linda

Alberto   **David**   **Linda**   **Marisa**

1. ¿Cómo se llama la mamá de Linda? *Susana Gajardo*
2. ¿Cómo se llama el papá de Linda? *Juan Gajardo*
3. ¿Cuántas hermanas tiene Linda? *Marisa*
4. ¿Cómo se llama su hermana? *Linda*
5. ¿Cuántos hermanos tiene Linda? *no*
6. ¿Cómo se llama la hermanita de David? *yes*

B. You want to find out about a classmate and his family, so you've prepared some questions.

PARTNER A: Ask the questions about your partner's family.

PARTNER B: Answer based on the members of your own family.

—¿Cómo te llamas? ¿Cuántos años tienes?
—**Me llamo (Juan Carlos Morales). Tengo diez años.**

1. ¿Cómo se llama tu papá?
2. ¿Cómo se llama tu mamá?
3. ¿Tienes hermanas? ¿Cuántas?
4. ¿Tienes hermanos? ¿Cuántos?
5. ¿Cuántos años tiene tu papá?

ENTRE AMIGOS

¿Cuántos hermanos tienes? Get together with three or four classmates. Take a class survey to see how many students have a certain number of brothers and sisters. Divide up the names of the people in your class so that each of you only has to ask a portion of your classmates. (Be sure to include yourselves.) Make a chart like this one to keep track of the responses. Write a check mark for each person who responds.

1 hermano _____
2 hermanos_____
3 hermanos_____
4 hermanos_____
5+ hermanos_____

Once your group has the information, make a bar graph to show the results, just like this one from Julia's group:

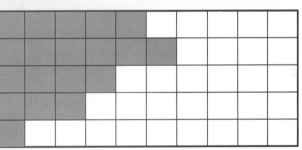

	1	2	3	4	5	6	7	8	9	10
1 hermano										
2 hermanos										
3 hermanos										
4 hermanos										
5+ hermanos										

Una familia en Buenos Aires, Argentina

¡Hablemos!

Who is who?

—¿Quién es el hijo de Sandra?

—Miguelito es el hijo de Sandra.

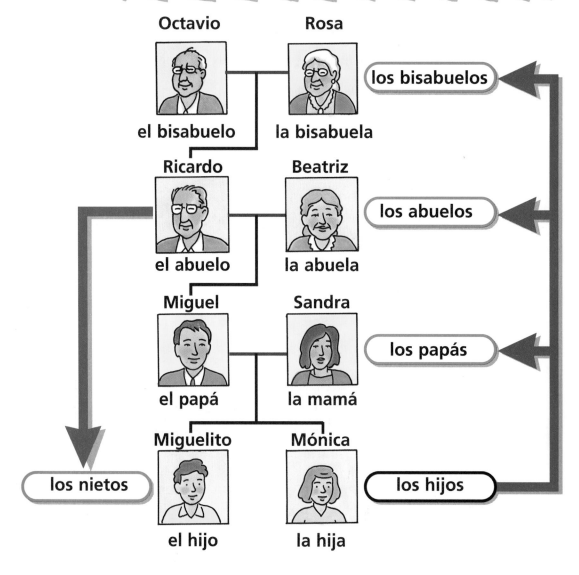

Octavio   **Rosa**

el bisabuelo   la bisabuela   los bisabuelos

Ricardo   **Beatriz**

el abuelo   la abuela   los abuelos

Miguel   **Sandra**

el papá   la mamá   los papás

los nietos   **Miguelito**   **Mónica**   los hijos

el hijo   la hija

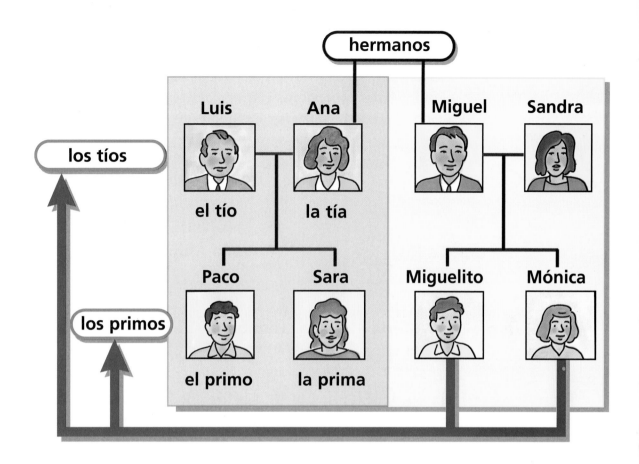

hermanos

los tíos

Luis — el tío
Ana — la tía

Miguel
Sandra

los primos

Paco — el primo
Sara — la prima

Miguelito
Mónica

—¿Quién es la tía de Mónica?

—Ana es su tía.

Así es... In Spanish-speaking countries, to show respect, it is customary to address older people or people in positions of authority as *Don* or *Doña*—*Don* for men and *Doña* for women. These terms are used with the person's first name, not the family name—*Don José, Doña Amalia.*

PRACTIQUEMOS

A. You're trying to tell your mother about the family of your friend, María. Your mom's getting confused, so you draw a family tree to help answer her questions.

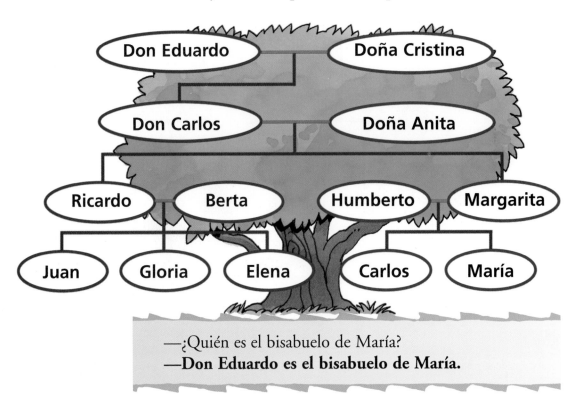

—¿Quién es el bisabuelo de María?
—**Don Eduardo es el bisabuelo de María.**

1. ¿Quién es el tío de María?

2. ¿Quién es la abuela de María?

3. ¿Quiénes son las primas de María?

4. ¿Quién es la nieta de Don Eduardo?

5. ¿Quién es el hijo de Berta?

6. ¿Quién es el hermano de María?

7. ¿Quiénes son los hijos de Don Carlos?

8. ¿Quién es la tía de Carlos?

B. Your brother comes into the room and you start to tell him who is who in María's family. Use the family tree on the previous page.

> Elena es _____ de Carlos.
> **Elena es la prima de Carlos.**

1. Berta es _____ de María.
2. Humberto es _____ de María.
3. Doña Anita es _____ de María.
4. Juan es _____ de María.
5. Gloria es _____ de María.
6. Ricardo es _____ de María.
7. Don Carlos es _____ de María.
8. Margarita es _____ de María.
9. Carlos es _____ de María.

C. Now your father is asking questions about María's family, but he's getting everyone mixed up.

PARTNER A: Ask the question about María's family.
PARTNER B: Answer no; then give the correct family relationship according to the family tree on the previous page.

> —¿Es Juan el hermano de María?
> **—No, Juan es el primo de María.**

1. ¿Es Berta la mamá de María?
2. ¿Es Carlos el hermano de Humberto?
3. ¿Es Doña Cristina la abuela de María?
4. ¿Es Ricardo el nieto de Don Carlos?
5. ¿Es Elena la hija de Doña Anita?
6. ¿Es Don Carlos el papá de Carlos?
7. ¿Es Humberto el papá de Gloria?
8. ¿Es Don Eduardo el hermano de Don Carlos?
9. ¿Es María la hermana de Elena?

ENTRE AMIGOS

You've just spent a year living with a very large family in Lima, Peru. Make a book about your Peruvian family to show your friends. Draw pictures of each person doing his or her favorite thing. Put the family tree on the inside cover.

When you're finished, get together with a small group of classmates and share information about your "family."

Es el papá. Se llama Miguel Prado.

Se llama Beti. Es la hija de Doña Rosa. Tiene ocho años.

Don David es el abuelo de Jorge. Él tiene seis hermanos.

¿Cómo lo dices?

Talking about who things belong to

Study these pictures and sentences. What word do you use to say that something belongs to you? What word do you use to say that something belongs to someone else?

¡Es **mi** perro!

¿Es **tu** perro?

Señor, ¿es **su** perro?

Es **su** perro.

Es **su** perro.

Use **mi** to talk about something that belongs to you. When you're talking to a friend about something that belongs to him or her, use **tu.** When you're talking to an adult or someone you don't know, use **su.** Finally, when you want to talk about something that belongs to someone else, either a boy or a girl, use **su.**

Now, how do you think these words change when you're talking about more than one of something? Look at these sentences.

Es **mi** primo.

Son **mis** primos.

Es **tu** abuelo.

Son **tus** abuelos.

¿Es **su** hija?

¿Son **sus** hijas?

All you have to do is add an **-s** to the word that shows possession. **Mi** becomes **mis**, **tu** becomes **tus**, and **su** becomes **sus**.

¿Tú vas con tu familia?

When you write, be sure not to confuse *tú* with *tu*. The accent mark makes the difference between saying *you* and *your*.

¡ÚSALO!

A. You and a friend are looking at a family album. You are trying to guess who is who in your friend's family.

PARTNER A: Ask a question using the first word.
PARTNER B: Answer with the second word.

¿hermano? / primo
—**¿Es tu hermano?**
—**No, es mi primo.**

1. ¿abuelo? / papá
2. ¿tía? / abuela
3. ¿hermana? / prima

4. ¿abuela? / mamá
5. ¿papá? / tío
6. ¿primo? / hermano

B. You and your friends are helping the teacher go through the lost-and-found box at school. You keep finding old, lost items. In each case, answer the question **¿Qué es esto?** with the information you see.

¿Qué es esto?  **Es mi bolígrafo.**

C. Your friend's father is showing you pictures. Ask him about the people in the pictures. Remember to use **su** or **sus** in your questions.

Señor, ¿es _____ abuelo?
Señor, ¿es su abuelo?

1. Señor, ¿son _____ primos?

2. Señor, ¿es _____ abuela?

3. Señor, ¿son _____ primas?

4. Señor, ¿es _____ mamá?

D. Your favorite young singer from Mexico is visiting. You want to learn about her family. Write five questions you would like to ask her. Look at these questions for ideas:

1. ¿Es grande o pequeña tu familia?

2. ¿Cómo se llama tu mamá?

3. ¿Va tu hermano a la escuela?

4. ¿Son alumnos tus hermanos?

5. ¿Vive tu abuela en una casa grande?

ENTRE AMIGOS

Find a partner. Choose one of the kids in this photograph to be your "brother" or "sister." Then decide on the names and relationships of everyone in the photograph:

Ana – prima, Luisa – abuela, Manuel – papá, Esteban – hermano, etc.

Your partner will ask you five questions about your "new family." Then change roles and ask your partner questions.

¿Es Manuel tu papá?

¿Son Ana y María tus hermanas?

¿Cuántos primos tienes?

¿Cómo se llama tu abuela?

¿Cómo lo dices?

Talking about special people and things

In Spanish, you can put endings on words to show that people or things are special to you. Find the special endings in these sentences.

Es mi **perrito**.

Son mis
abuelitos.

Es mi **casita**.

Son mis
hermanitas.

Did you notice the endings **-ito, -itos, -ita,** and **-itas?**

Adding these endings to people's names turns them into nicknames:

Juan va al cine.　　　　**Juanito** va al cine.
Adela estudia mucho.　　**Adelita** estudia mucho.
Luis escribe muy bien.　　**Luisito** escribe muy bien.
Pepe tiene un hermano.　　**Pepito** tiene un hermano.

These endings can also be used to say that something is small:

Leo mi **libro.**　　　　　　Leo mi **librito.**
Escribe en su **papel.**　　　Escribe en su **papelito.**
Él tiene una **casa** pequeña.　Él tiene una **casita.**

¡Úsalo!

A. Your friend is very affectionate with everyone in the family. How does he answer your questions?

PARTNER A:	Ask the question.
PARTNER B:	You're the friend. Answer using the correct ending.

—¿Tienes un hermano?
—**Sí, tengo un hermanito.**

1. ¿Tienes una abuela?
2. ¿Tienes una mamá?
3. ¿Tienes un hermano?
4. ¿Tienes dos primos?

5. ¿Tienes dos abuelos?
6. ¿Tienes una bisabuela?
7. ¿Tienes una prima?
8. ¿Tienes dos hermanas?

B. Carlos likes things that are small. How does he answer your questions?

—¿Lees un libro grande?
—**No, leo un librito.**

1. ¿Tienes un gato grande?
2. ¿Escribes en un papel grande?
3. ¿Te gustan los conejos grandes?
4. ¿Tienes dos pájaros grandes?
5. ¿Te gustan los loros grandes?
6. ¿Tienes una casa grande?

**Una mamá peruana
con su hijito**

C. Your friend always uses nicknames and talks about things as being small. It drives you crazy. Change all his sentences back to normal.

Miguelito tiene dos hermanitas.
Miguel tiene dos hermanas.

1. A Juanito le gustan los perritos.

2. Pepito escribe en su papelito azul.

3. Mi hermanito se llama Luisito.

4. Carlita tiene una casita gris.

5. Mi primita se llama Adelita.

6. La hermanita de Robertito se llama Juanita.

ENTRE AMIGOS

 Get together with a small group of your classmates. Create Spanish nicknames for yourselves and your other classmates.

When you are finished, share your nicknames with the class. See how many people have the same nicknames.

¡A divertirnos!

You'll soon be going on summer vacation! This game will help to remind you not to leave any of your things behind.

Get together with a group of 6–8 people. Use someone's backpack or a large bag. Each person in the group should include at least two different items they have at school, such as **un libro, un lápiz, una regla, un cuaderno,** etc. If your name is not on an item, write it on a piece of tape, and attach the tape to the item. For smaller items like **lápices,** put several together with a rubber band, and then attach the tape. Now everyone should put their items in the bag.

Get in a circle with your group. One person starts by reaching in the bag, pulling out an item, and asking **¿Qué es esto?**

The person to his or her left takes the item(s), looks at the name, and quickly responds:

Es mi regla. OR **Son tus bolígrafos.**
OR **Es su libro.** (pointing to the person)

Put the item aside, pass the bag to the left, and continue the game. The person responding must do so quickly. If you run out of items, put the ones you've used back in the bag.

Goodbye, and have a great summer! As we say in Spanish,

¡Hasta la vista!

APPENDIX

NOMBRES FEMENINOS

Adela, Adelita   Adele
Adriana   Adrian, Adrienne
Alberta   Alberta
Alejandra   Alexandra
Alicia   Alice
Amalia   Amelia
Ana   Ann, Anne
Andrea   Andrea
Ángela   Angela
Anita   Anita
Antonia   Antonia

Bárbara   Barbara
Beatriz   Beatrice
Berta   Bertha
Blanca   Blanche

Carla   Carla, Karla
Carlota   Charlotte
Carmen   Carmen
Carolina   Caroline
Catalina   Kathleen
Catarina
          Catherine, Kathryn
Cecilia   Cecile
Clara   Clara, Claire
Claudia   Claudia
Constancia   Constance
Consuelo   Connie
Corina   Corinne
Cristina   Christine

Débora   Deborah
Diana   Diana, Diane
Dolores   Dolores

Elena   Ellen, Elaine, Helen
Elisa   Lisa, Elise
Elsa   Elsa
Ema   Emma
Emilia   Emily
Esperanza   Hope
Estela   Estelle, Stella
Ester   Esther
Eugenia   Eugenia
Eva   Eve, Eva

Francisca   Frances

Gloria   Gloria
Graciela   Grace

Inés   Agnes, Inez
Irene, Irena   Irene
Isabel   Isabel, Elizabeth

Josefa   Josephine, Josie
Josefina   Josephine, Josie
Juana   Jane, Jean, Joan
Judit   Judith, Judy
Julia   Julia

Laura   Laura
Leonor   Eleanor
Lidia   Lydia
Linda   Linda
Lola   Lola
Lucía   Lucy
Lucinda   Lucinda, Lucy
Luisa   Louise, Lois

Margarita
          Margaret, Marguerite
María
          Mary, Maria, Marie
Mariana   Mary Ann
Marta   Martha
Matilde   Matilda
Mercedes   Mercedes
Mónica   Monica

Nora   Nora

Olga   Olga

Patricia   Patricia
Paula   Paula

Raquel   Rachel
Rebeca   Rebecca
Roberta   Roberta
Rosa   Rose
Rosalía   Rosalie

Sara   Sara, Sarah
Silvia   Sylvia
Sofía   Sophie
Sonia   Sonia
Susana   Susan, Suzanne

Teresa   Theresa
Taña   Tanya, Tania
Toña   Toni

Verónica   Veronica
Victoria   Victoria
Violeta   Violet
Virginia   Virginia

Nombres Masculinos

Abrahán Abraham
Adán Adam
Agustín Augustin
Alberto Albert
Alejandro Alexander
Alfredo Alfred
Andrés Andrew
Ángel Angel
Antonio Anthony
Arnaldo Arnold
Arturo Arthur

Benjamín, Benito
    Benjamin
Bernardo Bernard

Carlos Charles
Claudio Claude
Cristiano Christian

Daniel Daniel
Darío Darryl
David David
Diego James
Domingo Dominick
Donaldo Donald

Edmundo Edmund
Eduardo Edward
Emilio Emil
Enrique Henry
Ernesto Ernest
Esteban Stephen, Steven
Eugenio Eugene

Fabián Fabian
Federico Frederick
Felipe Phillip
Francisco Francis

Gabriel Gabriel
Gerardo Gerard
Gilberto Gilbert
Gregorio Gregory
Guillermo William
Gustavo Gustaf, Gus

Heriberto, Herberto
    Herbert
Hugo Hugo

Jaime James
Javier Xavier
Jeremías Jeremy
Jorge George
José Joseph
Josué Joshua
Juan John
Juanito Jack, Johnny
Julio Julius, Jules

León Leo, Leon
Leonardo Leonard
Lionel Lionel
Lorenzo Lawrence
Luis Louis

Manuel Manuel, Emmanuel
Marcos Mark
Mario Mario
Martín Martin

Mateo Matthew, Matt
Mauricio Maurice
Miguel Michael, Mike

Natán Nathan
Nicolás Nicholas

Óscar Oscar

Pablo Paul
Paco, Pancho Frank
Patricio Patrick
Pedro Peter
Pepe Joey, Joe

Rafael Ralph
Raimundo Raymond
Ramón Raymond
Raúl Raoul
Ricardo Richard, Rick
Roberto Robert
Rodolfo Rudolph
Rogelio Roger
Rolando Roland
Rubén Ruben

Samuel Samuel
Saúl Saul
Simón Simon

Timoteo Timothy
Tomás Thomas, Tom

Vicente Vincent
Víctor Victor
Virgilio Virgil

LOS NÚMEROS

0 cero	**34** treinta y cuatro	**68** sesenta y ocho
1 uno	**35** treinta y cinco	**69** sesenta y nueve
2 dos	**36** treinta y seis	**70** setenta
3 tres	**37** treinta y siete	**71** setenta y uno
4 cuatro	**38** treinta y ocho	**72** setenta y dos
5 cinco	**39** treinta y nueve	**73** setenta y tres
6 seis	**40** cuarenta	**74** setenta y cuatro
7 siete	**41** cuarenta y uno	**75** setenta y cinco
8 ocho	**42** cuarenta y dos	**76** setenta y seis
9 nueve	**43** cuarenta y tres	**77** setenta y siete
10 diez	**44** cuarenta y cuatro	**78** setenta y ocho
11 once	**45** cuarenta y cinco	**79** setenta y nueve
12 doce	**46** cuarenta y seis	**80** ochenta
13 trece	**47** cuarenta y siete	**81** ochenta y uno
14 catorce	**48** cuarenta y ocho	**82** ochenta y dos
15 quince	**49** cuarenta y nueve	**83** ochenta y tres
16 dieciséis	**50** cincuenta	**84** ochenta y cuatro
17 diecisiete	**51** cincuenta y uno	**85** ochenta y cinco
18 dieciocho	**52** cincuenta y dos	**86** ochenta y seis
19 diecinueve	**53** cincuenta y tres	**87** ochenta y siete
20 veinte	**54** cincuenta y cuatro	**88** ochenta y ocho
21 veintiuno	**55** cincuenta y cinco	**89** ochenta y nueve
22 veintidós	**56** cincuenta y seis	**90** noventa
23 veintitrés	**57** cincuenta y siete	**91** noventa y uno
24 veinticuatro	**58** cincuenta y ocho	**92** noventa y dos
25 veinticinco	**59** cincuenta y nueve	**93** noventa y tres
26 veintiséis	**60** sesenta	**94** noventa y cuatro
27 veintisiete	**61** sesenta y uno	**95** noventa y cinco
28 veintiocho	**62** sesenta y dos	**96** noventa y seis
29 veintinueve	**63** sesenta y tres	**97** noventa y siete
30 treinta	**64** sesenta y cuatro	**98** noventa y ocho
31 treinta y uno	**65** sesenta y cinco	**99** noventa y nueve
32 treinta y dos	**66** sesenta y seis	**100** cien
33 treinta y tres	**67** sesenta y siete	

WORD LIST

SPANISH-ENGLISH

The Spanish-English Word List contains the Spanish words you learn in each unit, as well as words you come across in readings. A number in parentheses indicates the unit where a word was taught. (B) indicates the **¡Bienvenidos!** *(Welcome!)* unit.

Here's a sample entry—a word and its English equivalent:

la **computadora** computer (B)

The bold letters in different type tell you that **computadora** is the entry. "La" tells you to use "la" (not "el") with **computadora**. (B) tells you that **computadora** first appears in the **¡Bienvenidos!** unit.

Here's another entry:

¡Hablemos! (com.; inf.: hablar)   Let's talk! (B)

The abbreviations in parentheses—*com.* and *inf.*—tell you that **¡Hablemos!** is a command, and that it comes from the word **hablar** (to talk).

Here are the complete Word List abbreviations:

Abbreviations

adj.	adjective	*inf.*	infinitive
adv.	adverb	*m.*	masculine
com.	command	*pl.*	plural
f.	feminine	*s.*	singular

A

a   to, at (6)

a casa   home (3)

¡A divertirnos!   Let's have fun! (1)

a la casa de Ana   to Ana's house (3)

a la una   at one o'clock (8)

¿A qué hora?   At what time? (8)

a tiempo   on time (8)

a veces   sometimes (6)

abril   April (6)

la **abuela**   grandmother (10)

el **abuelo**   grandfather (10)

los **abuelos**   grandparents (10)

aburrido, aburrida   boring (9)

adiós   good-bye (B)

¿adónde?   (to) where? (3)

¿Adónde vas?

Where are you going? (3)

agosto   August (6)

ahora   now (5)

al (*a+el*)   to the (3)

la **alumna**   (female) student (B)

el **alumno**   (male) student (B)

amarillo, amarilla   yellow (2)

la **amiga**   (female) friend (B)

las **amigas**   (female) friends (B)

el **amigo**   (male) friend (B)

los **amigos**   (male or male and female) friends (B)

entre amigos   among friends (B)

anaranjado, anaranjada

orange (color) (2)

el **animal** (*pl.: animales*)   animal (2)

el **aniversario**   anniversary (6)

el **año**   year (6)

el Año Nuevo   New Year (6)

¿Cuántos años tienes?

How old are you? (7)

los meses del año

the months of the year (6)

Tiene ochenta años.

He/She is eighty years old. (7)

aprender   to learn (9)

el **arte** (*m.*)   art (4)

así   so (B)

así, así   so-so (B)

Así es.   It's so. (1)

¡ay!   oh! ouch! (2)

azul   blue (2)

B

bailar   to dance (6)

la **bandera**   flag (1)

el Día de la Bandera   Flag Day (6)

la **biblioteca**   library (4)

bien   well (B)

Estoy bien.   I'm fine. (B)

muy bien   very well

¡Bienvenidos!   Welcome! (B)

la **bisabuela**   great-grandmother (10)

el **bisabuelo**   great-grandfather (10)

los **bisabuelos**   great-grandparents (10)

blanco, blanca   white (2)

el **bolígrafo**   ballpoint pen (1)

el **borrador**   eraser (1)

buen   good (*before a m. noun*) (5)

Hace buen tiempo.

The weather is good. (5)

bueno, buena   good (1)

¡Buenas noches!

Good evening! Good night! (B)

¡Buenas tardes!   Good afternoon! (B)

¡Buenos días!   Good morning! (B)

C

el **calendario**   calendar (3)

el **calor**   heat (5)

Hace calor.   It's hot. (5)

Tengo calor. I'm hot. (7)

caminar to walk (6)

el **canario** canary (2)

cantar to sing (4)

la **casa** house, home (3)

a casa home (3)

en casa at home (3)

celebras (*inf.: celebrar*) you celebrate (6)

la **cesta** basket (1)

las **ciencias** science (9)

ciencias sociales social sciences (9)

el **cine** movie theater, movies (3)

al cine to the movies (3)

el **círculo** circle (2)

claro clearly, of course (1)

¡Claro que sí! Of course! (1)

la **clase** class (B)

el salón de clase classroom (1)

el **coche** (*m.*) car (8)

el **color** (*pl.: colores*) color (2)

¿De qué color es?

What color is it? (2)

cómo how (B)

¿Cómo es...? What is...like? (2)

¿Cómo estás? How are you? (B)

¿Cómo lo dices?

How do you say it? (1)

¿Cómo se llama (el muchacho)?

What's the (boy's) name? (B)

¿Cómo te llamas?

What's your name? (2)

comprender to understand (9)

la **computadora** computer (B)

la clase de computadoras

computer class (4)

usar la computadora

to use the computer (4)

el **conejo** rabbit (2)

corto, corta short (2)

el **cuaderno** notebook (1)

el **cuadrado** square (2)

¿cuál? ¿cuáles? (*pl.*)

what? (B) which one? (5)

¿Cuál es tu número de teléfono?

What's your phone number? (B)

¿Cuáles son...? Which are...? (3)

¿Cuál te gusta?

Which one do you like? (5)

¿cuándo? when? (3)

¿cuánto? ¿cuánta? how much? (8)

¿Cuánto tiempo hay?

How much time is there? (8)

¿cuántos? ¿cuántas?

how many? (B)

¿Cuántos/Cuántas...hay?

How many...are there? (1)

¿Cuántos años tienes?

How old are you? (7)

¿Cuántos son...más...?

What is...plus...? (B)

el **cuarto** quarter (8)

un cuarto de hora

a quarter of an hour (8)

una hora y cuarto

an hour and a quarter (8)

el **cumpleaños** birthday (6)

¿Cuál es la fecha de tu cumpleaños?

When is your birthday? (6)

El cumpleaños de Marco es el...

Marco's birthday is... (6)

D

de of (1); in (8)

de la mañana

in the morning (8)

de la tarde

in the afternoon (8)

¿De qué color...? What color...? (2)

los **deportes** sports (4)

el **día**   day (3)

   ¡Buenos días!   Good morning! (B)

   el Día de la Bandera   Flag Day (6)

el **día de fiesta**   holiday (6)

diciembre   December (6)

difícil (*pl.:* ***difíciles***)   difficult (9)

divertido, divertida

   amusing, entertaining, fun (9)

el **dolor**   pain (7)

   Tengo dolor.   I have a pain. I'm in

     pain. (7)

el **domingo**   Sunday (3)

   los domingos   on Sundays (3)

¿dónde?   where? (3)

E

la **educación física**   physical education (9)

el (*m. s.*)   the (B)

él   he (6)

ella   she (6)

en   in (1)

   en punto   on the dot, sharp (*time*) (8)

enero   January (6)

entre   between, among (B)

   entre amigos   among friends (B)

es (*inf.:* ***ser***)   is (B)

escribir   to write (9)

el **escritorio**   teacher's desk (B)

la **escuela**   school (3)

el **español**   Spanish (9)

espectacular   spectacular (9)

la **estación**   season (5)

estar   to be (B)

   Está nevando.   It's snowing. (5)

   Está lloviendo.   It's raining. (5)

   Está nublado.   It's cloudy. (5)

estás (*inf.:* ***estar***)   you are (*s.*) (B)

   ¿Cómo estás tú?   How are you? (B)

esto   this (1)

¿Qué es esto?   What's this? (1)

estoy (*inf.:* ***estar***)   I am (B)

   Estoy muy mal.   I feel very bad.

     I'm not well. (B)

estudiar   to study (4)

F

fabuloso, fabulosa   fabulous (9)

fácil (*pl.:* ***fáciles***)   easy (9)

la **familia**   family (10)

fantástico, fantástica   fantastic (9)

favorito, favorita   favorite (2)

   ¿Cuál es tu animal favorito?

     What's your favorite animal? (2)

febrero   February (6)

la **fecha**   date (6)

   ¿Cuál es la fecha?

     What's the date? (6)

feliz   happy (6)

   ¡Feliz cumpleaños!

     Happy birthday! (6)

la **fiesta**   celebration, party (6)

   día de fiesta   holiday (6)

el **fin** (*pl.:* ***fines***)   end (3)

   fin de semana   weekend (3)

el **flamenco**   flamingo (2)

fresco, fresca   cool, fresh (5)

   Hace fresco.   It's cool (weather). (5)

frío, fría   cold (5)

   Hace frío.   It's cold (weather). (5)

   Tengo frío.   I'm cold. (7)

G

el **gato**   cat (2)

la **geografía**   geography (9)

el **gimnasio**   gymnasium (4)

el **globo**   globe (1)

Gracias.   Thank you. Thanks. (B)

Muchas gracias.

Thank you very much. (B)

grande   big (2)

la **gripe**   flu (7)

Tengo la gripe.   I have the flu. (7)

gris   gray (2)

gustar   to like (5)

Le gusta el verano.

He/She likes summer. (5)

Me gusta el libro.   I like the book. (5)

¿Qué te gusta hacer?

What do you like to do? (6)

¿Te gusta pintar?

Do you like to paint? (5)

H

¡Hablemos!

(*com.; inf.: **hablar***)   Let's talk! (B)

hacer   to do (4); it is (5)

Hace buen/mal tiempo.

The weather is good/bad. (5)

Hace calor.   It's hot. (5)

Hace fresco.   It's cool. (5)

Hace frío.   It's cold. (5)

Hace sol.   It's sunny. (5)

Hace viento.   It's windy. (5)

¿Qué hace Inés?

What's Inés doing? (5)

¿Qué tiempo hace?

What's the weather like? (5)

¿Qué vas a hacer?

What are you going to do? (4)

el **hambre** (*f.*)   hunger (7)

¡Tengo hambre!   I'm hungry! (7)

hasta   until (B)

¡Hasta luego!   See you later! (B)

¡Hasta mañana!

See you tomorrow! (B)

¡Hasta pronto!   See you soon! (B)

hay (*inf.: **haber***)   there is, there are (1)

¿Cuántos...hay?

How many...are there? (1)

¿Qué hay...?   What is there...? (1)

la **hermana**   sister (10)

las **hermanas**   sisters (10)

la **hermanastra**   stepsister (10)

el **hermanastro**   stepbrother (10)

el **hermano**   brother (10)

los **hermanos**

brothers, brothers and sisters (10)

la **hija**   daughter (10)

el **hijo**   son (10)

los **hijos**   children (10)

la **hoja**   sheet (1)

hoja de papel   sheet of paper (1)

¡Hola!   Hello! Hi! (B)

el **hombre**   man (B)

la **hora**   hour (8)

¿A qué hora?   At what time? (8)

¿Qué hora es?   What time is it? (8)

un cuarto de hora

a quarter of an hour (8)

una media hora   a half-hour (8)

hoy   today (3)

¿Qué día es hoy?

What day is today? (3)

I

importante   important (9)

la **independencia**   independence (6)

el Día de la Independencia

Independence Day (6)

el **inglés**   English (9)

interesante   interesting (9)

el **invierno**   winter (5)

ir   to go (3)

¿Adónde vas?

Where are you going? (3)

ir a (+ *inf.*) to be going to… (4)
    ¿Qué vas a hacer?
        What are you going to do? (4)
    Voy a… I'm going to… (4)

J

el **jueves** Thursday (3)
    los jueves on Thursdays
  julio July (6)
  junio June (6)

L

  la (*f. s.*) the (B)
el **lápiz** (*pl.:* ***lápices***) pencil (1)
  largo, larga long (2)
  las (*f. pl.*) the (1)
  le to him/her/you (5)
    le gusta he/she/you like (5)
la **lección** lesson (9)
  leer to read (9)
el **libro** book (1)
  llamas (*inf.:* ***llamar***) you call (B)
    Me llamo… My name is… (B)
    Se llama… His/Her name is… (B)
    Te llamas… Your name is… (B)
  Llueve. (*inf.:* ***llover***) It's raining. (5)
el **loro** parrot (2)
  los (*m. pl.*) the (1)
  luego later (B)
    ¡Hasta luego! See you later! (B)
el **lunes** Monday (3)
    los lunes on Mondays (3)
la **luz** light (B)

M

la **madrastra** stepmother (10)
la **madre** mother (6)

  el Día de la Madre Mother's Day
  mal (*adj., before a m. s. noun*) bad (B)
    Hace mal tiempo.
        The weather is bad. (5)
  mal (*adv.*) not well, badly (B)
    Estoy mal. I'm not well. (B)
la **mamá** mother, mom (10)
  mañana (*adv.*) tomorrow (B)
    ¡Hasta mañana!
        See you tomorrow! (B)
la **mañana** morning (8)
    de la mañana
        in the morning (A.M.) (8)
el **mapa** map (1)
  maravilloso, maravillosa
    marvelous, wonderful (9)
la **mariposa** butterfly (2)
  marrón (*pl.:* ***marrones***) brown (2)
el **martes** Tuesday (3)
    los martes on Tuesdays (3)
  marzo March (6)
  más plus (B)
    Cuatro más seis son diez.
        Four plus six is ten. (B)
las **matemáticas** mathematics (9)
  mayo May (6)
  me myself, to me (B)
    Me gusta… I like… (5)
    Me llamo… My name is… (B)
la **medianoche** midnight (8)
  medio, media half (8)
    una hora y media
        an hour and a half (8)
    media hora a half-hour (8)
el **mediodía** noon (8)
  mejores (*inf.:* ***mejorar***) get well (7)
    ¡Que te mejores! Get well! (7)
  menos to, of (time) (8)
    Son las dos menos cuarto.
        It's fifteen to two. (8)

el **mes** month (6)

¿En qué mes? (In) what month? (6)

la **mesa** table (1)

mí me, myself (7)

mi (*s.*) my (10)

el **miedo** fear (7)

Tengo miedo. I'm afraid. (7)

el **miércoles** Wednesday (3)

los miércoles on Wednesdays (3)

el **minuto** minute (8)

mis (*pl.*) my (10)

morado, morada purple (2)

la **muchacha** girl (B)

el **muchacho** boy (B)

mucho (*adv.*) a lot (4)

Estudio mucho. I study a lot. (4)

mucho, mucha (*adj.*) much (4)

Tengo mucha hambre.

I'm very hungry. (7)

Tengo mucho frío.

I'm very cold (7)

la **mujer** (*pl.: mujeres*) woman (B)

la **música** music (4)

muy very (B)

Muy bien, gracias.

Very well, thanks. (B)

N

nadar to swim (6)

la **Navidad** Christmas (6)

negro, negra black (2)

nevar to snow (5)

Está nevando. It's snowing. (5)

la **nieta** granddaughter (10)

el **nieto** grandson (10)

los **nietos** grandchildren (10)

Nieva. (*inf.: nevar*) It's snowing. (5)

Está nevando. It's snowing. (5)

no no (1)

la **noche** night, evening (8)

¡Buenas noches! Good evening! (B)

de la noche in the evening (8)

noviembre November (6)

los **novios** sweethearts (6)

el Día de los Novios

Valentine's Day (6)

nublado (*adj.*) cloudy (5)

Está nublado. It is cloudy. (5)

el **número** number (B)

¿Cuál es tu número de teléfono?

What's your phone number? (B)

nunca never (5)

O

octubre October (6)

el **oso** bear (2)

el **otoño** autumn, fall (5)

P

el **padrastro** stepfather (10)

el **pájaro** bird (2)

el **papá** father, dad (10)

los **papás** parents (10)

el **papel** (*pl.: papeles*) paper (1)

la hoja de papel

sheet of paper (1)

la **pared** (*pl.: paredes*) wall (1)

el **parque** park (3)

patinar to skate (6)

pequeño, pequeña small, little (2)

el **perro** dog (2)

el **pez** (*pl.: peces*) fish (2)

pintar to paint (4)

la **pizarra** chalkboard (B)

por in (8)

por la mañana in the morning (8)

por la noche in the evening (8)

por la tarde   in the afternoon (8)

¿Por qué?   Why? (9)

practicar   to practice (4)

   practicar los deportes

      to practice (play) sports (4)

   ¡Practiquemos!

      (*com.; inf.: **practicar***)

      Let's practice! (B)

la **prima**   (female) cousin (10)

las **primas**   (female) cousins (10)

la **primavera**   spring (5)

el **primero**   the first (of the month) (3)

el **primo**   (male) cousin (10)

los **primos**   (male or male and female) cousins
   (10)

la **prisa**   hurry (7)

   Tiene prisa.   He's/She's in a hurry. (7)

el **profesor**   (male) teacher (B)

la **profesora**   (female) teacher (B)

pronto   soon (B)

   ¡Hasta pronto!   See you soon! (B)

próximo, próxima   next (3)

   la próxima semana   next week (3)

la **puerta**   door (B)

la **puesta del sol**   sunset (8)

el **punto**   dot (8)

   en punto   on the dot, sharp (time) (8)

el **pupitre**   student's desk (1)

Q

¿qué?   what? (B)

   ¿A qué hora?   At what time? (8)

   ¿De qué color...?   What color...? (2)

   ¿Qué es esto?   What is this? (B)

   ¿Qué hay...?   What is/are there? (1)

   ¿Qué hora es?   What time is it? (8)

   ¿Qué tal?   How is it going? (B)

   ¿Qué tiempo hace?

      What's the weather like? (5)

¿Qué tienes?   What's the matter? (7)

   What do you have? (1)

¿Qué vas a hacer?   What are you
   going to do? (4)

¿quién?   who? (B)

   ¿Quién es...?   Who is...? (B)

R

el **ratón** (*pl.: **ratones***)   mouse (2)

la **raza**   race (6)

   el Día de la Raza   Columbus Day

la **razón** (*pl.: **razones***)   reason (7)

   tener razón   to be right (7)

el **rectángulo**   rectangle (1)

la **regla**   ruler (1)

el **reloj** (*pl.: **relojes***)   clock (1)

rojo, roja   red (2)

rosado, rosada   pink (2)

S

el **sábado**   Saturday (3)

   los sábados   on Saturdays (3)

sabes (*inf.: **saber***)   you know (B)

   ¿Sabes que...?   Do you know that...?

la **salida**   exit (8)

   la salida del sol   sunrise (8)

el **salón**   large room (1)

   el salón de clase   classroom (1)

la **salud**   health (9)

se   himself, herself, yourself (9)

   Se llama...   His/Her name is... (B)

la **sed**   thirst (7)

   Tengo sed.   I'm thirsty. (7)

la **semana**   week (3)

   el fin de semana   weekend (3)

   esta semana   this week (3)

   la próxima semana   next week (3)

   sensacional   sensational (9)

señor   Mister

el **señor**   man, gentleman

señora   Mrs., ma'am

la **señora**   woman, lady

señorita   Miss (B)

la **señorita**   young lady

septiembre   September (6)

ser   to be

   ¿Quién es?   Who is he/she? (B)

sí   yes (1)

   Sí, claro.   Of course. (1)

siempre   always (6)

la **silla**   chair (B)

el **sol**   sun

   Hace sol.   It's sunny. (5)

   la puesta del sol   sunset (8)

   la salida del sol   sunrise (8)

son (*inf.: ser*)   they are (B)

   Son las dos.   It's two o'clock.

su (*pl.: sus*)   his, her, your (10)

el **sueño**   sleep (7)

   Tengo sueño.   I'm sleepy. (7)

la **suerte**   luck (1)

   ¡Buena suerte!   Good luck! (1)

   Tengo suerte.   I'm lucky. (7)

T

tal   such (B)

   ¿Qué tal?   How are you doing? (B)

también   also, too (6)

la **tarde**   afternoon, evening (8)

   ¡Buenas tardes!

      Good afternoon! Good evening! (B)

   por la tarde   in the afternoon

      (P.M.) (8)

te   yourself, to you (B)

   ¿Cómo te llamas?

      What's your name? (B)

¿Te gusta?   Do you like it? (5)

el **teléfono**   telephone (B)

   el número de teléfono

      phone number (B)

tener   to have, to be (7)

   ¿Qué tienes?   What's the matter?

      What do you have? (7)

   tener… años   to be…years old (7)

   tener calor   to be hot (7)

   tener dolor   to have a pain (7)

   tener frío   to be cold (7)

   tener hambre   to be hungry (7)

   tener la gripe   to have the flu (7)

   tener miedo   to be afraid (7)

   tener prisa   to be in a hurry (7)

   tener razón   to be right (7)

   tener sed   to be thirsty (7)

   tener sueño   to be sleepy (7)

   tener suerte   to be lucky (7)

terrible   terrible (9)

la **tía**   aunt (10)

el **tiempo**   weather (5), time (8)

   a tiempo   on time (8)

   ¿Cuánto tiempo hay?

      How much time is there? (8)

   Hace buen/mal tiempo.

      The weather is good/bad. (5)

   ¿Qué tiempo hace?

      What's the weather like? (5)

la **tienda**   store (3)

tienes (*inf.: tener*)   you have (1)

el **tigre**   tiger (2)

el **tío**   uncle (10)

los **tíos**   uncles, aunts and uncles (10)

la **tiza**   chalk (1)

el **triángulo**   triangle (2)

tu (*pl.: tus*)   your (*informal*) (B)

tú   you (*informal*) (6)

U

un, una   a, an   (B)

la   **unidad** (*pl.:* ***unidades***)   unit   (1)

unos, unas   some, a few   (2)

usar   to use   (4)

    ¡Úsalo! (*com.; inf.:* ***usar***)   Use it!   (1)

    usar la computadora

       to use the computer   (4)

usted (*pl.:* ***ustedes***)   you (*formal*)   (7)

V

va (*inf.:* ***ir***)   he/she goes, is going;

     you go   (3)

vas (*inf.:* ***ir***)   you go   (3)

las   **veces**   times   (6)

    a veces   sometimes   (6)

la   **ventana**   window   (1)

el   **verano**   summer   (5)

verde   green   (2)

los   **veteranos**   veterans   (6)

    el Día de los Veteranos

       Veterans Day   (6)

el   **viento**   wind   (5)

    Hace viento.   It's windy.   (5)

el   **viernes**   Friday   (3)

    los viernes   on Fridays   (3)

voy (*inf.:* ***ir***)   I go, I'm going   (3)

    Voy al gimnasio.

       I'm going to the gymnasium.   (4)

Y

y   and   (B)

    ¿y tú?   How about you?   (10)

yo   I   (6)

WORD LIST

ENGLISH-SPANISH

This list gives English words with similar meanings to the Spanish words that you've learned in *¡Hola!* A number in parentheses or (B) indicates the unit where a word is taught.

A

a, an un, una (B)
afraid, to be tener miedo (7)
afternoon la tarde (8)
a lot mucho (4)
also también (6)
always siempre (6)
and y (B)
animal el animal (2)
anniversary el aniversario (6)
April abril (6)
art el arte (4)
August agosto (6)
aunt la tía (10)
autumn el otoño (5)

B

bad mal (*adj. before a m. s. noun*) (B)
ballpoint pen el bolígrafo (1)
basket la cesta (1)
bear el oso (2)
big grande (2)
bird el pájaro (2)
birthday el cumpleaños (6)
black negro, negra (2)
blackboard la pizarra (B)
blue azul (2)
book el libro (1)

boring aburrido, aburrida (9)
boy el muchacho (B)
brother el hermano (10)
brown marrón (2)
butterfly la mariposa (2)

C

calendar el calendario (3)
to **call** llamar (B)
canary el canario (2)
cat el gato (2)
to **celebrate** celebrar (6)
chair la silla (B)
chalk la tiza (1)
chalkboard la pizarra (B)
chalk eraser el borrador (1)
children los hijos (10)
circle el círculo (2)
class la clase (B)
classroom el salón de clase (1)
clock el reloj (1)
cold frío, fría (5)
cold, to be tener frío (5)
color el color (2)
computer la computadora (B)
cool fresco, fresca (5)
cousin (female) la prima (10)
cousin (male) el primo (10)

D

dad   el papá (10)

to **dance**   bailar (6)

date   la fecha (6)

daughter   la hija (10)

day   el día (3)

December   diciembre (6)

desk (pupil's)   el pupitre (B)

desk (teacher's)   el escritorio (B)

difficult   difícil (*pl*.: difíciles) (9)

dog   el perro (2)

door   la puerta (B)

E

easy   fácil (*pl*.: fáciles) (9)

end   el fin (*pl*.: fines) (3)

English   el inglés (9)

eraser   el borrador (1)

evening   la tarde (8)

exit   la salida (8)

F

fall   el otoño (5)

family   la familia (10)

fantastic   fantástico, fantástica (9)

father   el papá (10)

fear   el miedo (7)

February   febrero (6)

few, a   unos, unas (2)

fine   bien (B)

first, the   el primero (3)

fish   el pez (*pl*.: peces) (1)

flag   la bandera (1)

flamingo   el flamenco (2)

flu, to have the   tener la gripe (7)

Friday   viernes (3)

friend   el amigo, la amiga (B)

fun   divertido (9)

G

geography   la geografía (9)

girl   la muchacha (B)

globe   el globo (1)

to **go**   ir (3)

good   buen (*before a m. s. noun*), bueno, buena (B)

Good afternoon.   Buenas tardes. (B)

good-bye   adiós (B)

Good evening.   Buenas noches. (B)

Good morning.   Buenos días. (B)

Good night.   Buenas noches. (B)

grandchildren   los nietos (10)

granddaughter   la nieta (10)

grandfather   el abuelo (10)

grandmother   la abuela (10)

grandparents   los abuelos (10)

grandson   el nieto (10)

gray   gris (2)

great-grandfather   el bisabuelo (10)

great-grandmother   la bisabuela (10)

great-grandparents   los bisabuelos (10)

green   verde (2)

gymnasium   el gimnasio (4)

H

half   medio, media (8)

half-hour, a   una media hora (8)

happy   feliz (6)

to **have**   tener (7)

health   la salud (9)

he   él (6)

Hello!   ¡Hola! (B)

her   su (10)

Hi!   ¡Hola! (B)

his   su (10)

hot, to be   tener calor (7)

hour   la hora (8)

hour and a half, an   una hora y media (8)

hour and a quarter, an
    una hora y cuarto (8)
house   la casa (3)
how?   ¿cómo? (B)
  how many?   ¿cuántos...?
    ¿cuántas...? (B)
  how much?   ¿cuánto...? ¿cuánta...? (8)
hungry, to be   tener hambre (7)
hurry, to be in a   tener prisa (7)

I

I   yo (6)
important   importante (9)
interesting   interesante (9)
It's...   Es...; Está... (2)
  It's cloudy.   Está nublado. (5)
  It's cold.   Hace frío. (5)
  It's cool.   Hace fresco. (5)
  It's hot.   Hace calor. (5)
  It's raining.   Está lloviendo. Llueve. (5)
  It's snowing.   Está nevando. Nieva. (5)
  It's sunny.   Hace sol. (5)
  It's windy.   Hace viento. (5)

J

January   enero (6)
July   julio (6)
June   junio (6)

K

to **know**   saber (B)

L

large   grande (2)
to **learn**   aprender (9)
lesson   la lección (6)
library   la biblioteca (4)

light   la luz (B)
to **like**   gustar (5)
little   pequeño, pequeña (2)
long   largo, larga (2)
luck   la suerte (1)
lucky, to be   tener suerte (7)

M

man   el hombre (B)
map   el mapa (1)
March   marzo (6)
marvelous   maravilloso, maravillosa (9)
mathematics   las matemáticas (9)
matter?, What's the   ¿Qué tienes? (7)
May   mayo (6)
me   me (7)
midday   el mediodía (8)
midnight   la medianoche (8)
minute   el minuto (8)
Miss   Señorita (B)
mom   la mamá (10)
Monday   lunes (3)
month   el mes (6)
morning   la mañana (8)
mother   la madre (6); la mamá (10)
mouse   el ratón (2)
movie theater   el cine (3)
music   la música (4)
my   mi (*s.*), mis (*pl.*) (10)
  My name is...   Me llamo... (B)
myself   me (7)

N

never   nunca (6)
New Year   el Año Nuevo (6)
new   nuevo, nueva (B)
next week   la próxima semana (3)
night   la noche (8)
noon   el mediodía (8)

notebook el cuaderno (2)
November noviembre (6)
now ahora (5)
number el número (B)

O

October octubre (6)
of de (1)
  Of course! ¡Claro que sí! (1)
orange (color) anaranjado,
  anaranjada (2)

P

pain, to be in, to have a
  tener dolor (7)
to **paint** pintar (4)
paper el papel (1)
parents los papás (10)
park el parque (3)
parrot el loro (2)
pen (ballpoint) el bolígrafo (1)
pencil el lápiz (1)
physical education
  la educación física (9)
pink rosado, rosada (2)
to **play sports** practicar los deportes (6)
to **please** gustar (5)
plus más (B)
to **practice** practicar (4)
purple morado, morada (2)

Q

quarter-hour, a un cuarto de hora (8)

R

rabbit el conejo (2)
to **read** leer (9))
rectangle el rectángulo (2)
red rojo, roja (2)

right, to be tener razón (7)
ruler la regla (1)

S

Saturday sábado (3)
school la escuela (3)
science las ciencias (9)
season la estación (5)
See you later. Hasta luego. (B)
See you soon. Hasta pronto. (B)
See you tomorrow. Hasta mañana. (B)
sensational sensacional
  (*pl.*: sensacionales) (9)
September septiembre (6)
she ella (6)
sheet of paper la hoja de papel (1)
short corto, corta (2)
to **sing** cantar (4)
sister la hermana (10)
to **skate** patinar (6)
sleep el sueño (7)
sleepy, to be tener sueño (7)
small pequeño, pequeña (2)
to **snow** nevar (5)
social sciences las ciencias sociales (9)
some unos, unas (2)
sometimes a veces (6)
son el hijo (10)
soon pronto (7)
so-so así, así (B)
Spanish el español (9)
sports los deportes (4)
spring la primavera (5)
square el cuadrado (2)
stepbrother el hermanastro (10)
stepfather el padrastro (10)
stepmother la madrastra (10)
stepsister la hermanastra (10)
store la tienda (3)
student (female) la alumna (B)
student (male) el alumno (B)

student's desk   el pupitre (1)

to **study**   estudiar (4)

summer   el verano (5)

sun   el sol (8)

Sunday   domingo (3)

sunrise   la salida del sol (8)

sunset   la puesta del sol (8)

to **swim**   nadar (6)

T

table   la mesa (1)

teacher   (male) el profesor, (female) la profesora (B)

telephone   el teléfono (B)

telephone number   el número de teléfono (B)

terrible   terrible (9)

thanks   gracias (B)

the   el (*m. s.*), la (*f. s.*), los (*m. pl.*), las (*f. pl.*)

there is, there are   hay (1)

thirsty, to be   tener sed (7)

this week   esta semana (3)

Thursday   jueves (3)

tiger   el tigre (2)

time   el tiempo, la hora (8)

today   hoy (3)

tomorrow   mañana (3)

too   también (6)

triangle   el triángulo (2)

Tuesday   martes (3)

U

uncle   el tío (10)

to **understand**   comprender (9)

until   hasta (B)

to **use**   usar (4)

V

very   muy (B)

W

to **walk**   caminar (6)

wall   la pared (1)

wastebasket   la cesta (1)

weather   el tiempo (5)

Wednesday   miércoles (3)

week   la semana (3)

weekend   el fin de semana (3)

Welcome!   ¡Bienvenidos! (2)

well   bien (B)

what?   ¿qué? (1)

what color?   ¿de qué color? (2)

what time?   ¿a qué hora? (8)

when?   ¿cuándo? (3)

where?   ¿dónde? ¿adónde? (3)

which?   ¿cuál? (5)

white   blanco, blanca (2)

who?   ¿quién? (1)

whose?   ¿de quién? (10)

why?   ¿por qué? (9)

wind   el viento (5)

window   la ventana (1)

winter   el invierno (5)

woman   la mujer (B)

to **write**   escribir (9)

Y

year   el año (6)

years old, to be   tener...años (7)

yellow   amarillo, amarilla (2)

yes   sí (1)

you   (informal) tú; (formal) usted (pl. *ustedes*) (7)

INDEX

Acknowledgments

The publisher would like to thank the following photographers, organizations, and individuals for permission to reprint their photographs.
The following abbreviations are used to indicate the locations of photographs on pages where more than one photograph appears: T (top), B (bottom), L (left), R (right), and M (middle).

Cover Photographer:
Robert Keeling

Studio Photographers:
Jerry White Photography, Inc.
P&F Communications

Eduardo Aparicio: 112; **Stuart Cohen:** 25M, 103B, 141T, 149, 153, 156, 158, 169, 193, 223; **COREL Professional Photos CD-ROM:** 107, Andrew Blaisdell; 159, William P. McElligott; **Steven Ferry:** 25B, 36, 45M, 60, 67T, 85B, 87, 123B, 187B, 203; **Manuel Figueroa:** 205; **Robert Fried:** 3T, 3M, 3B, 9, 14, 16, 45B, 71, 88, 93, 118, 123T, 129, 136, 137, 138R, 155, 163T, 167, 173; **Beryl Goldberg:** 22, 35, 67M, 72, 82, 91, 123M, 141B, 163M, 187TL, 189, 206, 209T, 209B, 213; **Alejandro Manosalva:** 30, 42, 67B, 73, 141M; **Mabel Niño:** 85T, 170; **Odyssey Productions/Chicago:** 103T, Robert Frerck; **Chip and Rosa María de la Cueva Peterson:** 138L, 147, 152, 163B, 204, 209M; **Ann Purcell:** 45T; **Carl Purcell:** 48, 52, 62, 96, 103M, 183; **Stock, Boston:** 51, Thomas R. Fletcher; 111, David J. Sams, Texas Imprint; **UNICEF:** 41; **World Vision:** 25T

Note: The publishers have made an effort to contact all copyright holders for permission to use their works. If any other copyright holders present themselves, appropriate acknowledgement will be arranged for in subsequent printings.